SUGAR ISLAND SAMPLER

"Necessity is the mother of ..." Abe Laramie's Model-T powered raft (drawing by Judy Bostater, copyright Media Exchange, Inc. Sandusky, OH.)

SUGAR ISLAND SAMPLER:
A SLICE
OF
UPPER PENINSULA HERITAGE

BY
BERNIE ARBIC

Bernie Arbic

Original Edition by:
The Priscilla Press, Allegan Forest, Michigan, 1992

Copyright 1992 and 2020 by Bernard Arbic

All rights are reserved. No portion of this publication may be reproduced without the express permission of the author.

Please direct any questions or comments concerning this publication to:
Bernie Arbic, 118 E. 6th Avenue, Sault Ste. Marie, MI. 49783

Front cover drawing by Joel B. Arbic based on a photograph of Charley Andrews taken by Bill Hamilton.

Back cover map image courtesy of Barry Lawrence Ruderman Antique Maps www.RareMaps.com

Cover design by William Gerrish

Satellite image on half title was taken June 2, 1976. I.D. # NASA ERTS E-2497-15400-7. Courtesy of U.S. Geological Survey Office. (Photographs available from the U.S. Department of the Interior, U.S. Geological Survey, EROS Data Center, Sioux Falls, S.D.).

Quotes on Pages 111 and 112 are reprinted from *The Diary of Bishop Frederic Baraga* edited by Regis M. Walling and Rev. N. Daniel Rupp by permission of Wayne State University Press
(Copyright 1990 by the Bishop Baraga Association and Archives).

ISBN 9798635633786

First Printing 1992
Second Printing 1993
Third Printing 2002
Fourth Printing 2006
Fifth Printing 2011
Expanded Edition 2020
The fourth, fifth, and Expanded Edition printings are under the auspices of the Chippewa County Historical Society, **www.cchsmi.com**

To "Pete" and Pearl Arbic - my parents and Sugar Islanders

"All dressed up to go to town."

TABLE OF CONTENTS

Foreword 11

Preface 13

I. Early History & Navigation 15

II. Early Island Economy 42

III. Ferries & Roads 57

IV. The Island People 71

V. Island Institutions 97

VI. More Recently 130

VII. In Conclusion 144

Expanded Edition Material 146

Sugar Island Facts 172

References 174

Index 177

Foreword

From the moment you drive onto the Sugar Island Ferry you know you have embarked on an adventure, a visit to a place time has been kinder to than most, a relaxing spot lacking many of the irritating complexities of modern life - a land where residents look deep into a stranger's eyes and if they like what they see are quick to present the hand of friendship.

I first ventured a ride on that ferry in July, 1984. I had come to the island to spend the weekend with my friend and fellow historian Roger Pilon. Little did I suspect but that weekend would change my life forever.

Pilon's place, situated on the north side of the island close to Brassar Point, was a rendezvous, it seems, for a colorful coterie of Sugar Islanders. It was there I met Brian Belleau, the fiddler of the Sugar Island Boys band; Tom Stevens, affable captain of the Sugar Island Ferry and another of the Sugar Island Boys; big Burt Shipman and several others who would become my friends. And it was there, hoeing in a garden she shared with Pilon, that I met the love of my life.

That July weekend, with Sugar Island at its loveliest, passed in a blur as we paddled a canoe to Lake George, explored one of the nearby smaller islands, bumped along island roads on bikes, talked incessantly and fell in love. Two weeks later I asked my Sugar Island princess to marry me.

That summer I got to know the island better as we toured interminable dusty roads, walked the twisting path through the woods to Chase Osborn's retreat on Duck Island, swam in the St. Marys, devoured "Big C" burgers at Clyde's Drive-In and downed drafts at the Hilltop Bar. She took me to other eastern U.P. places that were special to her: the beach at Pendill's Creek, Monocle Lake, the Indian Cemetery high on a bluff overlooking Bay Mills, Grand Marais and the nearby log slide. But Sugar Island remained my favorite, a haunting place with a mystique all its own, its heritage a rich tapestry of Chippewa warriors, French Canadian voyageurs, Yankee entrepreneurs and Finnish immigrants, woven by the great watery thoroughfare that flows past its shores.

But it was the Sugar Islanders who embraced the stranger from "Down Below" that cemented my love of the Island and its people: Honey McCoy, a snaggle-toothed, wonderful old piano player as sweet as his name; Rene Cote', one of the finest fiddlers in the North Country, a Canadian for whom Sugar Island was a second home; deep - voiced Joe Menard with a heart of gold; his wife Rose, whose hospitality is such that she would fry delectable fish into the wee hours as long as there was one mouth in the crowd that could swallow another bite; and Joe's mother Rosie, who, among the many other accomplishments of her long life, as an octogenarian demonstrated a hoochie-coochie strip dance to an audience of folklorists in Lansing.

That first Sugar Island summer was the best of my life and when autumn painted the banks of the St. Marys crimson and gold I married the woman the island had given me. We held our wedding reception at the Sugar Island Township Hall, a glorious pig roast to which half the islanders came. And you can be sure the Sugar Island Boys played their best.

Over the succeeding years, we have returned many times to Sugar Island and it has become even dearer to us. When we learned of Bernie Arbic's manuscript on the history of Sugar Island we leaped at the chance to publish it so that his fine research may perpetuate a heritage as colorful as that of any of Michigan's many insular gems.

It is with great pride that the Priscilla Press presents *Sugar Island Sampler: A Slice of Upper Peninsula Heritage.* The Priscilla Press, by the way, takes its name from the lovely lady I found on Sugar Island, my wife and partner, Priscilla.

Larry B. Massie
Allegan Forest, Michigan

The Sugar Island Boys at the first "Fiddler's Jamboree" 1982, in Sault Ste. Marie (courtesy Priscilla Massie)

Preface

Near the Straits of Mackinac, when people say "the island," they mean Mackinac Island; in the De Tour area, "the island" refers to Drummond for most folks. For me, "the island" will always mean Sugar Island.

Islands seem to be very special to those who have spent any length of time on them. Perhaps the same could be said about most any chunk of land, whether it is surrounded by water or not; but the fact that an island is surrounded by water makes it different in the sense that its boundary is not man-made, but natural and unmistakable (and sometimes uncrossable).

Part of the reason that islanders feel strong ties to one another has to derive from the absolutely clear-cut definition of where an island begins, and where it ends. If you start out at your home on the island, and can walk to Joe's place without getting wet, then Joe is an islander too.

I spent a good deal of time on Sugar Island during my childhood and youth; I developed a fascination for islands in general during that time, and I have visited quite a few since, over the years. Three years ago, I became aware of the existence of several small books which cover the local history of such Eastern Upper Peninsula communities as Kinross Township, Trout Lake, Drummond Island and others. Nothing similar had been done on Sugar Island, so I decided to write such a book in the fall of 1989. I began by interviewing some of the older residents or former residents of the island, recording the interviews on tape in most cases. Many had old photographs that are of general interest, and you will find some of them in the book.

Besides interviews, I began delving into records at the institutions and offices acknowledged below. It has been an enjoyable project for me. What a great opportunity it gives to call someone you don't know, and spend some time talking about the way things used to be. I am indebted to the people listed below; I thank them for their time and willingness to share memories (and in some cases, photos). I hope the book meets the following three goals:

1) To summarize and make more readily available some interesting information about the island, past and present.

2) To preserve some of the little known, everyday sorts of things that might otherwise be lost — especially contributions to the island's development by various individuals.

3) To stimulate an interest in the island's past, especially among those born and raised here, those who have adopted it as their home later in life, and those who have established summer homes on the island.

Thanks to the following people, who have helped me out in various ways : Mary L. Adams, Tom Allen, Joe Andrews, Pauline Andrews, Leslie Atkins, Dan and June Boyer, Louise Bretz, Pete Causley, Emery and Donna Corbiere, Gail Corbiere, Jeanette Corbiere, Royce and Impi Curlis, Albert Currie, Lloyd Drury, Lee Eitrem, Jack Fox, Reg and Agnes Fox, Reeta Freeborn, Angus Gurnoe, Chuck Gustafson, Bill Hamilton, Ken Hatfield, Lawrence and Sylvia Hokkanen, Sylvia Hovey, Marshall Hunt, Abe Laramie, Father Joseph Lawless, Marie Maleport, Bill Marks, George and Mary Ellen Marks, John Matheson, Irene McCoy, Joe Menard, "Chum" Menard, Rose Menard, Mary Murray, Jennylee Olesek, Jo Osmar, Bernice Payment, Yvonne Peer, Ed Pine, Howard Preslan, Allie Rogers, Virginia Roy, Bill and Nancy Saunders, Jane Schaeffer, Dorothy Sebastian, Melvin "Mooney" Sebastian, Carl and Pauline Secrest, John and Jeanne Shibley, Lawrence Tate, Adelaide Thibert, Alex Vuori, Henry Webster and John Wellington.

Thanks are also due the following organizations: Bayliss Public Library, Chippewa County Clerk's Office and Register of Deeds Office, Chippewa County Road Commission, Eastern Upper Peninsula Transportation Authority, Lake Superior State University Library and the Sugar Island Lions Club.

Special thanks to Allan Swanson for many helpful discussions about island history, for providing me with some specific sources of information, and for reading the manuscript as it neared its final stages. He offered encouragement, as well as many suggestions that improved the writing.

For the 2020 Expanded Edition, I wish to add the following names of people who have helped: Sue Anderson, Bernadette and Roger Azevedo, Phil Bellfy, Kim Gravelle, Rob Laitenen, Kathy Loup, Roger Pilon, George Snider, and Tom Van Dorn.

Special thanks to Connie Pim, for her delightful "Letter from a Ferry Grandmother," and extensive suggestions for the coverage of the Sugar Island Historical Preservation Society, to Bill Gerrish for his beautiful cover design, and to Connie Thompson, who did the layout for the new edition.

I have tried to be as accurate as possible in recording names and dates; I hope the inevitable errors are few in number and not too serious. Sugar Island is a big place, a fact of which I am more aware after having written this book! This is not a comprehensive history — but I have attempted to make it balanced and representative.

I. Early History & Navigation

Sugar Island is situated in the St. Marys River near its northern end, in the eastern Upper Peninsula of Michigan. First, we'll take a look at the island itself, from the vantage point of a satellite.

The satellite image of the island and surrounding area appearing on the half-title page was taken in June, 1976. Roads that slice through the dark, forested land show up nicely, as do farm clearings created in the late nineteenth and early twentieth centuries. The higher proportion of farmland on the mainland both east and west of the island is noticeable. (see the petition on page 35 relating to farmland). Roads are an obvious indication of the development of the island, and so are the clearings, most of which are probably not natural. Since the half-title image shows distinctions between shallow and deep water, in some areas you can see where shipping channels have been dredged. This is especially true in the southern third of Lake George, where the channel stands out clearly. Note also the straight channel in the Little Rapids area. (The map on page 16 can be used to determine locations I refer to here and elsewhere in the book). If a satellite image could have been taken, for example, in 1776, when the island and surrounding water were in their natural states, and compared to the 1976 image, there would be some significant differences. One of the most striking would be in the Little Rapids area, as is discussed in more detail later.

I asked my colleague Ernie Kemp, professor of geology at Lake Superior State University, for a brief description of island geology and what follows is a summary of what he told me.

Bedrock underneath Sugar Island is part of a large layer of sedimentary rock called Jacobsville sandstone, which extends eastward from the Keweenaw Peninsula through the Upper Peninsula, and into Ontario. The portion underlying Sugar Island was either more resistant to erosion than the surrounding bedrock, or was perhaps thicker. One of these two reasons explains the existence of the island. The many boulders on the island, and the gravel and sand depositions were laid down by retreating glaciers about 15,000 years ago, creating an island with an area of almost 50 square miles, and with about 51 miles of frontage on the St. Marys River and Lake George, the name given to that branch of the river east of the island.

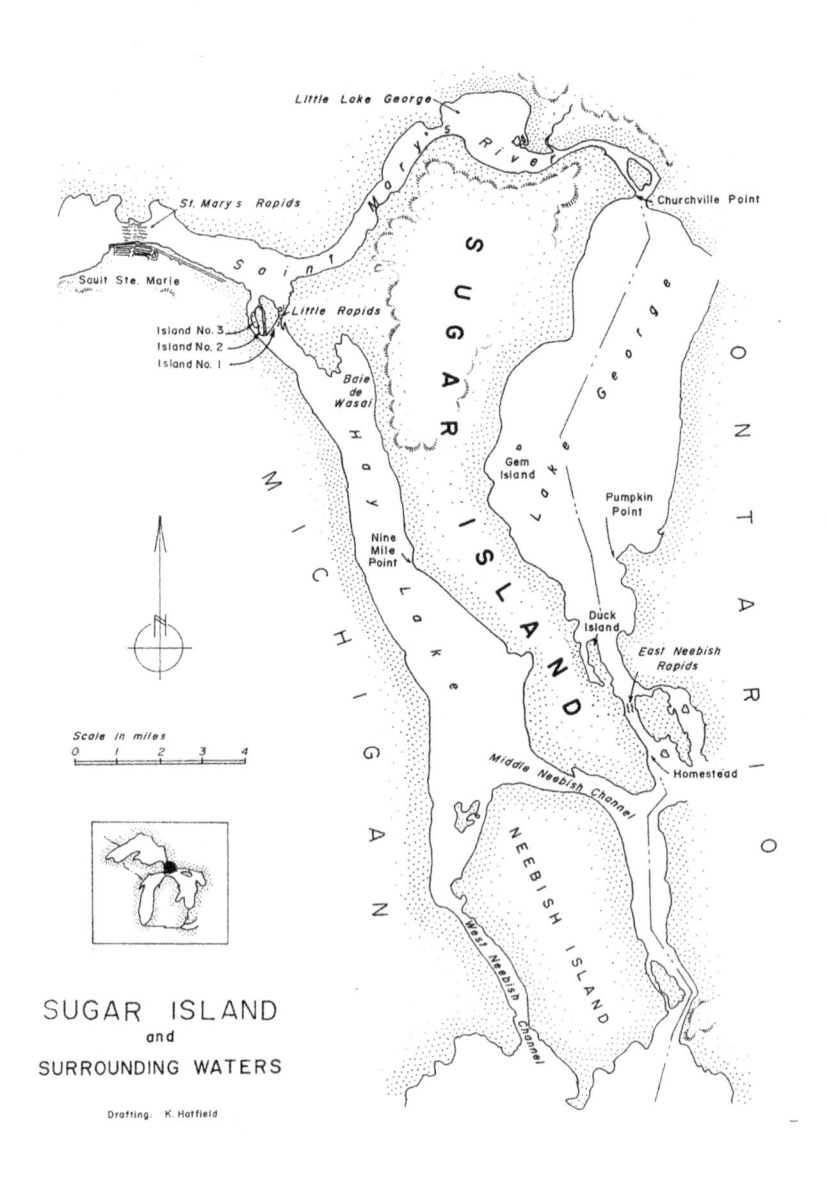

Map of Sugar Island and surrounding waters, based on a map in **The Illustrated Atlas of Sault Ste. Marie, Michigan and Ontario,** *published in 1888.*

The island has been known by at least three names in the relatively recent past. Native Americans of the area evidently referred to it as Sisibakwato Miniss in Chippewa, or "Sugartree Island", referring to their source of maple sugar. On a French map dated 1744, it shows up as ile St. George, and on British maps it was called St. George's Island as late as 1840; we still have a remnant of that name to the east of the island - Lake George. Incidently, on that early French map, St. Joseph's Island is shown as Ile St. Joseph, and Drummond Island as Ile du DeTour; Neebish Island is unnamed, but on later maps it was called St. Tammany's Island, and Squirrel Island (the small island northeast of Sugar Island) was known as Jonas' Island.

Sugar Island might still be known as St. George's today if a lengthy dispute over its ownership had been resolved in favor of Britain instead of the United States. The Treaty of Paris, signed by the United States and Britain in 1783, dealt with establishing the boundary between the U.S. and what is now Canada. Curiously, although most of the boundary is carefully defined in the treaty, it does not deal with the St. Marys River portion. According to Joseph Bayliss in *The River of Destiny*, this omission has never been satisfactorily explained, and appears to have been an oversight. However, the general principle implied by the treaty was that the boundary should be determined by a "navigable channel" in connecting waters such as the St. Marys River. As described in detail below, when the river was in its natural state, the desire to have the boundary follow a navigable channel supported the U.S. claim to Sugar Island.

Ownership of the islands in the St. Marys River had not been clearly established up to the time of the War of 1812. The Treaty of Ghent in 1814 made provision for determining exactly where the boundary between the U.S. and Canada would lie, from the St. Lawrence River on the east to the Mississippi on the west. Major Joseph Delafield, who was responsible for documenting the geography of the boundary waters, wrote the following in 1826, concerning Sugar Island:

> The claim of the United States is founded on the facts, that the only navigable channel is on the Canadian side of the island, and that the island or its greater proportion, is on the American side of the 'middle of the river', in any sense of that expression. The British claim has no other foundation than their strong desire to possess it. The island is about six-

teen miles in length, is two miles below Fort Brady, and of value for its sod and timber, but more especially because it binds the (Lake George) channel to the St. Marys Falls. Our claim to it has been sustained by ample evidence, and, I am gratified to add, however desirable amicable decisions are, that the American commissioner has rather made this island a point of disagreement than cede it to the British.

The issue was not finally settled until 1842, by the Webster-Ashburton Treaty - so the ownership of the island was in dispute for about sixty years after the Treaty of Paris. A much fuller account of the determination of the international boundary in the St. Marys River can be found in the book, *The Unfortified Boundary*, from which the above quotation was taken.

Some indication of the uncertain status of Sugar Island with regard to the boundary may be inferred from the following description of the island, found in the *Gazetteer of the State of Michigan* by John T. Blois, published in Detroit in 1838:

Sugar Island is one of the largest islands in the St. Marys Strait, and belongs to the British.

The peaceful resolution of the boundary dispute was held up as an example for the world to follow during the campaign to get the United Nations to locate its headquarters on the island -see chapter six.

The waters surrounding Sugar Island have been changed dramatically from the natural state that existed when Major Delafield made his survey. The navigable route in those days was by way of "the old channel" east of the island, through Lake George. Canoes and small boats drawing three to four feet of water (up to six feet, by some accounts) could pass to the west of Sugar Island, but to do so they had to deal with two sets of rapids. Thus, larger boats heading upriver towards the Sault took the longer route, through Lake George. This required passing through rapids as well, at the foot of the lake. The rapids were called "The Ship Neebish Rapid" on a chart dated 1822, drawn by Lt. Henry Bayfield of the British Royal Navy. Bayfield, "Lake Superiors's first modern cartographer" helped survey the Canadian shores of all the Great Lakes beginning in 1815. His manuscript map of Lake Superior, in particular, is extremely detailed and accurate. Born in Hull, England, in 1795, with little formal education he succeeded in rising to the rank of admiral in the British Navy. The portion of the shipping channel below the locks, between Sault Ste. Marie, Michigan and Sault Ste. Marie, Ontario, is referred to as the "Bayfield Channel" on Corps of Engineers charts. Bayfield, Wisconsin, also honors his memory. Soundings of 7 feet or more are given for the water in these rapids, although the inset from the chart, showing a detail of the rapids, indicates that "12 feet of water can be carried up the east side." The book *Sault Ste. Marie and Its Great Waterway* by Otto Fowle includes a portion of a letter written June 17, 1836, by Gabriel Franchere of the American Fur Company to his counterpart in Detroit. The letter is a plea that ships loaded with supplies in Detroit and bound for the Sault not be loaded to draw as much as eight feet - if they were loaded to that depth, they risked being grounded in these rapids or the "flats" at the south end of Lake George. Franchere describes such a grounding, with the costly and time consuming job of unloading part of the cargo to lighten the ship, then reloading it when the vessel had made it to deeper water.

In the days prior to any improvements to the channel, once upbound boats got into Lake George, they evidently followed a natural channel up the eastern side of the lake. Bayfield's 1822 chart indicates foundations of a storehouse and wharf that had existed at an earlier time, about three quarters of a mile west of the Canadian shoreline, and about one and one quarter miles north of Pumpkin Point. The natural channel on the east side of the lake passed just west of those foundations.

In 1856, Michigan Senator Lewis Cass introduced a bill to appropriate $100,000 for channel deepening in Lake George. President Pierce vetoed it, but his veto was overridden, and Captain Amiel Weeks Whipple was put in charge of the project. The following quotations are from *Essayons: A History of the Detroit District U.S. Army Corps of Engineers* by John W. Larson:

> Captain Whipple meanwhile had left Detroit aboard the steamer *Northstar* at 11:30 the night of July 3 [1857], with the subagent Mr. M.C. Dunnier, enroute for Lake George.... Arriving at Lake George on July 5, they employed a boat crew of Indians and made camp by building a hut of spruce tree branches on a small island on the west side of Lake George named Gem Island.

Larson's account doesn't say how long Whipple and his men remained camped on Gem Island, or why they chose to stay there rather than on Sugar Island proper. (Fewer mosquitoes?) They may later have camped at nearby Whipple Point, which undoubtedly was named after the captain.

Channel and harbor improvements throughout the Detroit District (which the Sault was part of) from the mid 1800's to 1975 are described in the book, and much of the material deals with the St. Marys River and the Sault Locks. The following paragraph is a summary of Larson's description of the dredging carried on in Lake George by Captain Whipple and his crew.

The original plan was to deepen the "west" channel through the flats at the south end of Lake George. Soon after his crew began surveying that route, the Indian men working for him told him of a better route, more toward the middle of the lake. After Whipple surveyed that possibility, he was convinced that the middle route was indeed far better. He sought permission to change the route, but it was not given. The remainder of the summer was spent dredging the west channel at a cost of $10,000 - thus using ten percent of the appropriation. In March, 1858, Captain Whipple went to Washington to make another appeal to change the route. Only after circumventing his superiors and writing directly to the Secretary of War was a three man commission appointed to settle on the best route. On May 20, 1858, this commission recommended the middle channel; a joint resolution of the U.S. Congress authorized the Secretary of War to use the remainder of the appropriation for channel work on the route which was best, in his judgment. On June 10, Captain Whipple received a telegram in Detroit directing him to abandon work on the west channel, and commence improving the middle channel. Dredging of this route took place from June 12 to November 6, 1858; by that time, a channel 14 to 15 feet deep and about 120 feet wide had connected the deep water portions at both ends of Lake George. Work resumed after iceout in 1859, and continued until the $100,000 was exhausted - by which time the channel through Lake George was 14 to 18 feet deep, and 150 feet wide almost throughout its length. In the East Neebish Rapids, the channel was 80 feet wide and 14 feet deep. Work in the rapids involved removal of 300 cubic yards of rock. Because sand washed back into the channel in Lake George, when further dredging work commenced after the Civil War, the crews found that in many places the depth was no more than 12 feet.

Joseph Bayliss, in *Historic St. Joseph's Island* notes that in 1875 "the Rains brothers" (Allen and Norman) built the propeller *St. Mary* at the south end of the island. The *St. Mary* was used as a lighter, helping boats across the Lake George Flats by taking on part of their cargo on one side of the flats and reloading it when the boat had crossed them. Smaller lighters had been used before that time for the same purpose. Groundings were apparently not uncommon in that area, if boats were loaded too optimistically, as mentioned earlier. By 1883 the Lake George channel had been deepened to 16 feet, which made the Rains' lighter unnecessary. This channel, by the way, is the one that is visible in the half-title satellite image discussed earlier in the chapter.

Steamer Glengarry *and consort* Minnedosa *in Little Lake George, probably about 1892. The* Minnedosa *was the only four-masted schooner of Canadian registry to sail the Great Lakes. The* Minnedosa *sank in 1905 (courtesy Bill Hamilton).*

The river around Sugar Island is quite narrow in places, particularly near Payment at the north end of the island, and through the East Neebish Rapids area. In such close quarters, it must have been an imposing sight when a steamboat passed by. The *Glengarry* was 180 feet long by 26 feet wide, and she was quite a bit smaller than some of the steamboats which used the old channel. For example, the *Brazil* was 276 feet long and 40 feet wide; the *Athabasca* was 263 feet long and 38 feet wide.

Meanwhile, the Canadian government also did a considerable amount of dredging in the south end of Lake George. The Canadians had spent about $200,000 there by 1884, when the Corps of Engineers and their Canadian counterparts agreed that the best long-term plan was to concentrate on opening a channel through Hay Lake, along the west side of Sugar Island. Suggestions that such a route be opened had arisen shortly after the first lock was built at the Sault, since it would shorten the trip through the St. Marys River by about 11 miles. Dredging had already begun by 1882.

Before the Hay Lake Channel had been completed, a serious collision occurred in the old channel. In October, 1891, the steamer *Susan E. Peck*, downbound with 60,000 bushels of wheat, sank and blocked the channel in Lake George as a result of a collision with the upbound schooner *George W. Adams*, light and in tow of the steamship *Aurora*. The accident took place in the early afternoon, about 1500 feet south of the "elbow" in the channel; that is, east and slightly south of Gem Island. The channel is narrow there, and the collision evidently happened because both vessels were too close to the center of the channel as they passed. An unnamed observer of marine affairs at the time was quoted in the October 17, 1891 issue of "*The Sault News*" thusly:

> There is no doubt in my mind that the accident was caused by hoggishness of the captain of the *Aurora* or the captain of the *Peck* or both... I have time and again noticed this hoggishness, both in the St. Clair and Sault rivers. The trouble is, the masters, especially of the big freighters, want every inch of room in the rivers, and do not want to give way... In these two rivers in the past five years have been sunk the propellers *Pontiac*, *Ohio*, *S.E. Peck*, *Quebec*, and schooners *Tasmania*, *S.J. Tilden*, *M.E. Tremble*, and *Helena*, all by collision... If all these collisions happen now in the daytime what will happen in the future when the Sault river is lighted and navigation is carried on at night?

In that era, commercial vessels plying the upper lakes were much smaller, but there were many more of them than there are today. Because the *Peck* was blocking the channel, traffic began backing up on both sides of her.

Before the blockade was cleared up, about 75 vessels were anchored above her in Lake George, and an equal number below - all costing their owners money. The Dunbar and Sullivan Dredging Company had several dredges nearby, working on the new channel west of Sugar Island, and it was decided that the quickest way to open the passage would be to dredge a temporary channel around the *Peck* and then deal with raising her. In about 4 days, the dredging crews, working round the clock, managed to open 600 feet of new channel around the *Peck*, 60 feet wide and 16 feet deep. (Dunbar and Sullivan was paid $12 per hour for each dredge). After the blockade was cleared, it took about eight days for the *Peck* to be raised, and towed for repairs.

Susan E. Peck *blocking channel in southern portion of Lake George (courtesy U.S. Army Corps of Engineers, photo by W.J. Bell).*

***Dredges working on temporary channel around the* Peck** *(courtesy of Chippewa County Historical Society, photo by W.J. Bell).*

The Weitzel Lock, completed in 1881, was the first lock to permit nighttime operations. This increased the desirability of having navigation lights on the St. Marys River. Even though construction of the Hay Lake Channel was underway, lights were built on the Lake George Channel in 1892, intended for use for only a few years. In a "*Sault News*" article dated Aug. 12, 1893, Locks Superintendent E.S. Wheeler compared the lighting of the Lake George route around Sugar Island with the lighting of the Hay Lake Channel then being built, which has fewer turns:

> The river range lights (Lake George Channel), of which there are fifteen sets, are intended as temporary, while those on Hay Lake, where only five sets will be required, will be built for permanent.

Allen Rains, about whom more is written in Chapter 4, tended some of the range lights near the south end of Sugar Island around the turn of the century. Jim Rains, Allen's grandson, accompanied his grandfather several times as he looked after the lights. Jim described the lights and procedures to me recently:

> The range lights were solid-mounted lamps, always on firm land - never in or close to the channel. There was a small shed-like enclosure on a plank or concrete platform. On this was built a house about six feet square. It contained a can of kerosene, holding about ten gallons. There was some cotton waste and a cleaning cloth. It was kept locked.
>
> Over this house, but mounted on the same platform, was a trestle of planks about eighteen feet high, somewhat like a pyramid. On top was a small frame, with a mast about three feet high topping it. The mast had a heavy steel eyelet near its top with a block and tackle attached. The lower block dropped through the pyramid-like frame and was attached to the lamp, which could then be raised.
>
> The lamp itself was large and heavy. It was always oil-fired. Servicing was only done once a week. One lowered the lamp, which was about four feet high and weighed about two hundred pounds; the cylindrical lens was cleaned, the wick was trimmed, the oil-chamber filled, and the lamp was hauled back up to the top of the trestle. All of this took about an hour, including policing the cabin.
>
> Range lights were never turned off during the navigation season. They would burn day and night for several weeks if need be. They were serviced by members of the U.S. Lighthouse Service.

In 1892, about fifteen lights and lighthouses were built along the old channel in Lake George and Little Lake George; some were on Sugar Island while others were floating lights, or were built on cribs. There were five lights on Lake George: Churchville Point Light, on Sugar Island at Churchville Point; Church Point Crib Light (rebuilt in 1896), southeast of Churchville Point; Upper Lake George Floating Light, northeast of Gem Island; Middle Lake George Crib Light, northwest of Pumpkin Point and Lower Lake George Float Light (rebuilt in 1895), west of Pumpkin Point.

One of the keepers of a light out in Lake George (probably the Church Point Crib Light) was David Sebastian. His son "Mooney" told me that his father used to be taken by tug to the light and left with two weeks of supplies. After two weeks, a relief man would be brought out and the cycle would be repeated.

I haven't been able to determine exactly when the lighthouses on Lake George were taken out of service. Since most commercial traffic began using the Hay Lake Channel as soon as it was completed in 1894, it seems likely that the lights were abandoned soon thereafter, but the fact that two of them were rebuilt in 1895 and 1896, after the Hay Lake Channel opened, indicates that at least some traffic continued to use the "Old Channel" at night for a few years. The lights are indicated on a chart dated 1898, but they are not shown on that same chart when it was updated in 1908.

Lighthouse in Lake George, ca. 1900 (courtesy Bill Hamilton).

As mentioned earlier, larger boats were prevented from sailing up the west side of Sugar Island, through Hay Lake, by two sets of rapids. The first set was the Middle Neebish Rapid, between Sugar and Neebish Islands. Bayfield's chart of 1822 shows these rapids to be about 2 miles long, with soundings of 3 to 6 feet. The second set was known as the Little Rapids, or the Sugar Island Rapids; the head of these rapids was near where the ferry now crosses— and in the area now known as the Little Rapids Cut. The appearance of the river near there at that time is preserved in a chart prepared from a survey done in 1825 by the same Lt. Bayfield. That chart contains the following description of these rapids:" fall estimated about 2 feet; 4 feet of water can be carried through". A detail of the area, taken from a chart prepared in 1853, is reproduced here to show the configuration of the islands prior to the dredging of the Little Rapids Cut. The two largest islands depicted are known as islands number 1 and number 2 (Island number 2 is also known as "Steere's Island.") The engineering drawing given later shows the portions of those islands that were removed when the Little Rapids Cut was dredged to complete the present, or "Hay Lake" shipping channel.

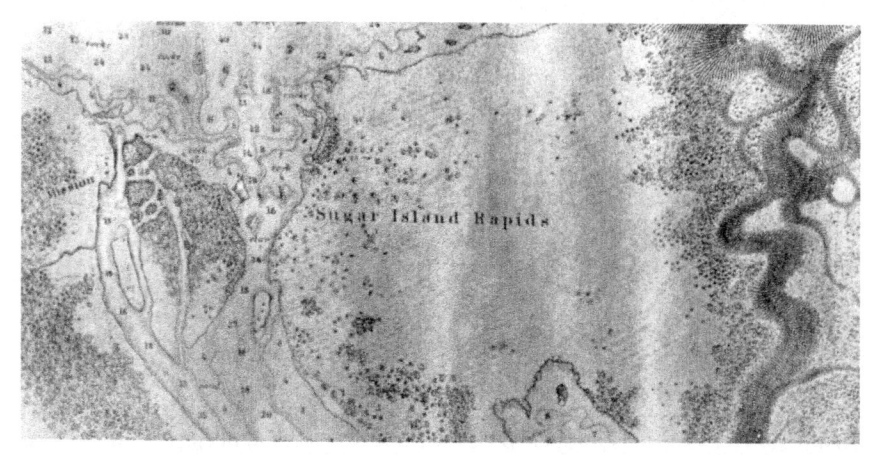

Detail of Little Rapids area, from a chart entitled "River Ste. Marie," prepared under the direction of J.N. Macombe 1853 (courtesy of U.S. Army Corps of Engineers).

The Dunbar and Sullivan Dredging Company began work on the Hay Lake Channel in 1882, at the Middle Neebish Rapids. Because the area was quite remote at the time, the men on the dredging crews lived on the *Packet*; a floating boarding house that could sleep fifty men. There was a large dining room on the *Packet*; a photograph of it in the Chippewa County Historical Society collection shows a room much nicer than the exterior of the building would suggest. Apparently, the cooks on the *Packet* were, appropriately, Mr. and Mrs. Frank Cook.

Living quarters for dredging crews on the Middle Neebish project in the 1880s, with the steam yacht **Bertie** *along side. There were evidently several stoves aboard, one of them listing heavily (courtesy Chippewa County Historical Society).*

The steam yacht *Bertie* was used to transport men and supplies to and from Sault Ste. Marie. Note the angled stovepipe near the peak of the *Packet*. The last names of the eight men at the end of the building were, from left to right, Neff, Squires, Cook, Young, Skelden, Ireland, McFarland, and Haentges. This information was preserved by F.E. Dunbar, who was captain of the *Bertie* on the project. He donated the pictures, with accompanying historical notes, to the Chippewa County Historical Society in 1953.

The dipper dredge Brian Boru *at work in the Middle Neebish Channel, ca.1880s (courtesy Chippewa County Historical Society).*

In 1889, dredging began in the Little Rapids area. The accompanying drawing shows the configuration of islands prior to the operation. Five and one-half acres of Island No. 2 were purchased from J. H. Steere in March of 1889 and 32.5 acres of Island No. 1 from F. Perry and E.A.G. Bryan the following June. The original channel was dredged to a width of 300 feet, and a depth of 20 feet; in the process, Island No. 1 was cut in two pieces. In 1893, a dike 2300 feet long was built between Sugar Island and Island No. 1. This was done to compensate for the increased flow through the newly dredged channel at Little Rapids Cut, in order to maintain the water level above the cut. This dike very likely became the base of the existing causeway from the island to the ferry dock. About 100 men worked on the dredging project during the final stages, according to a newspaper article of the day.

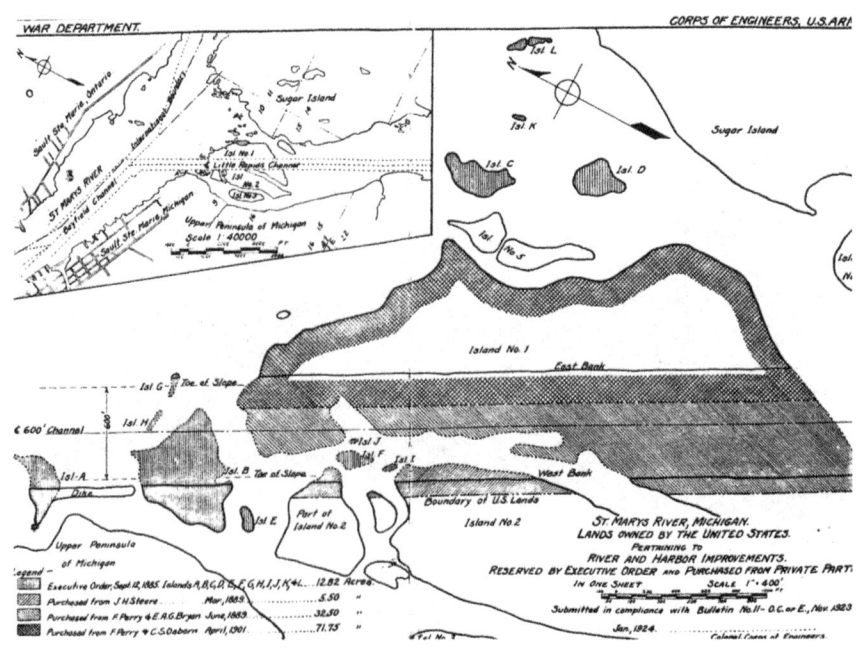

Detail of island configuration and channel course, Little Rapids Cut (courtesy U.S. Army Corps of Engineers).

Incidentally, when the *Susan E. Peck* was blocking the old channel in 1891, as described earlier, one steamboat managed to avoid the delay. A story in the October 17, 1891 issue of "*Sault News*" stated that:

> The steambarge *O.O. Carpenter* has the honor of being the first freight boat through the new channel. It was guided up the channel by Pilot Rains.

The "Pilot Rains" referred to is probably Owen Rains, from Sailor's Encampment on Neebish Island. Although it was not officially opened until 1894, evidently enough dredging had been completed by the fall of 1891 to allow a steamboat with an experienced pilot to make it up the new channel.

Coast Guard records indicate that 2,347,000 cubic yards of material were removed from the Little Rapids area between 1889 and 1895. Cost of the project is given by Larson in *Essayons* as $2,165,000.

Hay Lake Channel at Little Rapids in 1895, one year after the channel opened (courtesy U.S. Army Corps of Engineers, photo by W.J. Bell).

The Hay Lake channel was opened to shipping in June of 1894; in 1901, the remainder of Island No. 1 was purchased from F. Perry and Chase Osborn, and by 1904 the Little Rapids channel had been widened to the present 600 feet and deepened to 21 feet. By this time, according to Larson, 5 million cubic yards had been removed. That would be enough material to form a cubical "mountain" about 500 feet on each side. Perhaps a better comparison would be to note that it would require about 125 trips of a typical 1,000 foot lake carrier such as those that pass regularly through the cut today, to haul the material away.

How different this area would have looked before all this work was done! It would be nice to have an old photograph of the area before the Little Rapids Cut was dredged. There was a Chippewa village on the mainland at Little Rapids, or Neebeetung as it was called then. A Methodist Mission was established there about 1830. The Rev. John Pitezel was in charge of the mission in 1843, and described the site in his journal *Lights and Shades of Missionary Life*, published in 1859:

> It was two miles down the river from Fort Brady. At the station [the Mission Church], a large branch of the river breaks off abruptly, from the main channel, flowing southwardly, studded with numerous beautiful islets. The current here is very rapid; hence the name of Little Rapids.... The shore is very abrupt in front of the mission, the water being, a few feet from the land, eight or ten feet deep, and perfectly clear and transparent.... Lining the shore were about a dozen Indian houses, several wigwams, and the schoolhouse.

A description of an upbound passage by canoe through this part of the river is contained in the journals of the Cass Expedition in 1820. The journal was kept by James Doty, who would later win fame as one of the founders of the state of Wisconsin. The expedition party came up the St. Marys River in four large birch bark canoes - two of them with a carrying capacity of 3 tons of men and cargo. Quoting from Larson's book, *Essayons*:

> ...they reached the swift and shallow waters of the Neebish Rapids. There they managed to ascend fully loaded, against the strong current,

but their canoes were damaged. They had to stop at the head of the rapids, unload, and make repairs.

That evening, two miles below Sault Ste. Marie, they reached the swift but less steep Neebeetung Rapids, which they traversed, fully loaded and without damage, but with great difficulty. "For ten minutes", Doty wrote, "our canoe with all men at oars and paddles did not stir three feet either way."

Peter White, later to become one of Marquette, Michigan's most prominent citizens, passed through the area on his way to Marquette in 1849, when Little Rapids was in its natural state. In 1905 (after the channel had been dredged through Little Rapids,) he was chairman of the Semi-Centennial Celebration of the Sault Locks, and in an address for that occasion he described his 1849 passage as follows:

... When we reached the Sault, we found a place very few here would recognize, though many old landmarks persisted here not many years ago. The rapids were the same, as to the central fall, but the lands and buildings have very much altered the appearance of things, and the Hay Lake cut, especially down by the Little Rapids, almost more than all.

According to older islanders, it was possible to ford a team and wagon across the river at the Little Rapids prior to the opening of the Hay Lake Channel. This would have involved picking one's way among the islands and through the shallower parts of the rapids. As noted above, the current was extremely strong; it would be nice to have a first-hand account of such a crossing. Ed Pine told me that his grandfather, Ed Boulley, used to have a team made up of one horse and one ox. "Grandpa used to have to switch the team around for the return trip to the island, because it worked best to have the ox on the upstream side to hold against the current."

All indications in print are that small boats drawing no more than five to six feet of water were able to navigate the Little Rapids in its natural state. The tug *Pioneer*, built by Philetus and J. Wells Church at Church's Point on Sugar Island in 1864 was reported to have been the largest tug to run the Hay Lake Channel before its improvement, and it had a draft of six feet. Thus, it would seem that any attempt to ford the river from the mainland to Sugar Island would have required crossing a stretch of water at least six feet deep, contending with a strong current. However, the compensating dam above the main rapids, which now controls the flow of water through the rapids completely, was not finished until 1921, so the amount of water reaching Little Rapids was not regulated prior to that time. Perhaps seasonal variations in the flow rate would have allowed the fording of the river to have been accomplished at certain times of the year, while not at other times. Rev. Pitezel's journal contains the following entry which describes a boat in Little Rapids prior to the dredging:

> A fishing boat went down this morning, and one up this afternoon, laden with fish, towing an empty boat. The boatmen had to wade and pull the boat up the Little Rapids. But they comforted themselves by swearing they would get drunk at night.

So the evidence is mixed. Crossings with team and wagon might have taken place from time to time, under the right conditions - but it seems unlikely that they occurred with any regularity.

Residents of the island wanted to improve the link with the mainland, and the Hay Lake channel clearly affected that link. In the minutes of the Chippewa County Board of Supervisors, May 11, 1889, the following appears:

> The following petition signed by thirty-four rate (tax) payers of the Township of Sugar Island was received and read in: To the Hon. Board of Supervisors of Chippewa County, Michigan — we the undersigned taxpayers of the Township of Sugar Island do hereby pray that your Hon. body will allow the Township of Sugar Island to borrow the sum of $1,000 for the purpose of completing the county road running from big Lake George to Little Rapids which is partly made and as said road is the only hopes of us getting an outlet to the mainland by bridge or ferry and as said road would bring us in close proximity of the City of Sault Ste. Marie and as there is no bonded indebtedness on our township we do hereby pray that your Hon. body allow us to bond our township for one thousand dollars for ten years paying the interest annually on the

first day of March in each and every year and your Honorable servants as in duty bound will ever pray.

The permission was granted. Then on March 18, 1890 the following appears in the Board minutes:

A petition for a bridge between Sugar Island and the mainland was read and on a motion of Supervisor Johnston resolved that the county clerk be instructed to correspond with the Secretary of War through Gen. A. M. Poe as to the possibility of obtaining permission to cross the Hay Lake ship channel with a swing (bridge).

This motion also carried. An editorial in "*The Sault News*" dated March 22, 1890 supported the islanders' petition as follows:

The bridge which the Sugar Island people petitioned the Board of Supervisors for, is a matter of very great importance to the people on the Island, and of not a little interest to the people of the Soo. Sugar Island contains some of the best farming lands in the country; and yet, while land no farther from the Soo, but not cut off by water passage, are held at from $75 to $100 per acre, lands on the Island have little or no sale at from three to five dollars per acre. Nor is the cause for this state of things to seek. During a portion of the year when navigation is closed, this Island is cut off from market, either for selling produce or buying supplies... The Hay Lake Channel improvement cuts off any effective action by the Board of Supervisors at the present time, but they acted wisely in ordering the matter referred to the war department through General Poe... Since it is not proposed to make use of the bridge during the season of navigation, it is believed that the necessary permission can be obtained without great difficulty.

I've been unable to locate anything that may have come of that correspondence with General Poe. It's safe to say it would be a far different process today to alter a river in such a dramatic fashion, with the environmental impact statements that would need to be filed. Other than the items men-

The motor boat Clyde, which operated mainly between Drummond Island and De Tour. Note the "U.S. Mail" designation on the bow (courtesy of John Wellington).

tioned above, no other references to public discussion of the effect of the Hay Lake channel project on Sugar Island residents have come to my attention.

The only bridge there has ever been to Sugar Island is the ice bridge Mother Nature makes each winter, so a variety of boats were used to transport people and goods to and from the island before the ferry came into being.

Among the earliest named boats providing passenger service to Sugar Island from the Soo are the *Willamette* and the *Neon,* the latter having belonged to a Mr. LaBorde. About 1912, small craft with the names *Ferro*, *Aloha* and *Leora M.* are listed as having been converted from fish tugs to vessels providing passenger service to Sugar Island. These boats were operated by Elmo Kibby. Another boat operated on the St. Marys River between the Soo and DeTour was the *Clyde*. This boat was built by Francis Xavier Payment, who lived on Sugar Island before moving to the Soo. The *Clyde* was sunk in 1908 after having been struck by a steamboat.

In 1922 the small motorboat *Search* operated from a dock at the foot of Elm Street in the Soo, carrying passengers to and from Payment, on the north end of the island. A map prepared in 1926 by the Michigan Department of Conservation and called the Land Economic Survey shows "Payment Ferry Dock" near the foot of Mission Street in Sault Ste. Marie. (I am indebted to Father Edward J. Dowling for this information, contained in an unpublished article which I obtained from Dan and June Boyer).

The passenger and freight steamship *Elva* operated in the St. Marys River from 1896 to 1923, according to an article in the September/October, 1973 issue of *Telescope* magazine, from which the following information has been taken. For most of that twenty-seven year period, she was operated by Arnold Transit Line, and ran between the Soo and Mackinac Island. Between 1922 and 1923, she was sold to other owners, who operated her between the Soo and DeTour.

Under both owners, she evidently stopped at Willwalk and at the Rain's dock at the south end of Sugar Island. The article tells the interesting story of *Elva's* beginnings: she was built in 1889 as the *Glad Tidings*, a "gospel ship" used by Captain Henry Bunday to carry out missionary work in ports on Lake Michigan. Bunday had been involved in such missionary work for quite a few years prior to 1889 because the vessel built in 1889 was the fourth in a series of boats which all bore the name *Glad Tidings*. With his health failing, in 1896 he sold the steamship to James Knightly, who renamed her and began the St. Marys River Service noted earlier. After running the routes on the St. Marys River, the *Elva* operated between Mackinac Island, Mackinaw City, Cheboygan, and Les Cheneaux Islands until 1939. She finished her career as a barge to Mackinac Island.

The *Elva* was intentionally burned off Mackinac in 1954; this last episode in her career was to have been part of the official ground breaking ceremonies for the building of the Mackinac Bridge, but bad weather caused that part of the ceremony to be delayed.

Steamer Elva *(courtesy Rev. Edward J. Dowling).*

Marshall Hunt of the Soo told me that his family has had a summer home in the Payment area since 1921. He remembers the *Ferro*, which in those days went to Payment each evening and back to the Soo the next morning. Marshall said, "After school let out in the spring, we went down to our cottage for the summer. Mother shaved the hair off my head, and we didn't go back to town until the day before school started."

"Mooney" Sebastian remembers his parents going to town from their home in Payment. The family boat was a combination rowboat-sailboat with a centerboard. "They had two pairs of oars, and it was a long day to go to the Soo and back, depending on how much help they got from the sail," he recalled.

Several people have told me that some folks living on the west side of the island used to "catch a tow" uptown on a passing freighter. This would be after the Hay Lake Channel was opened. They would go out to the channel and edge up to the stern of the boat, hoping that an obliging crewman would throw them a line, as they evidently did often. (Ah, the good old days, imagine what insurance companies nowadays would think of that practice!) Angus Gurnoe told me that he remembers as a boy having to hide under the front deck of their boat when catching a tow - evidently the steamer crewmen were reluctant to tow a boat with children in it. His father had a friend in the Coast Guard who would sometimes ask a ship captain to tow them back downriver as well. Sometimes small boats going upriver to the Sault even locked through with their benefactor, and went "up the line," to camp on the shores of Whitefish Bay and pick blueberries during season.

Larry Hokkanen told me that the *Elva* would actually stop in midriver if hailed by someone in rowboat, and allow a passenger to board her in between stops. I've always thought it's great that the Algoma Central Railway train will stop out in the middle of nowhere if a passenger flags the train down, but you used to be able to do that on the river as well. He indicated that even some of the smaller ore boats passing by would lower a ladder and allow someone to clamber aboard for a lift up to the Sault, which he did more than once when working on the deepening of the Middle Neebish Channel in the early thirties.

Leslie Atkins lived at Baie de Wasai from 1904 to 1914. His father Alex ran the store at the Baie and was the first postmaster there. He told me about a sailboat owned by a Mr. Cadreau and operated out of the Baie: "He could load two horses on that boat, keeping one on each side of the center.

Sometimes he paired up the sailboat with a small gasoline powered launch. When the wind was favorable, the sailboat towed the launch, and when it wasn't, the launch towed the sailboat."

Alex Atkins sold his store at the Baie to Gene Thibert in 1914. To supply the store, Mr. Thibert used a launch which he named after his wife, Bertha.

Bertha Thibert and son Bobby in Gene Thibert's launch **Bertha**, *in the early 1930s (courtesy Jo Osmar).*

Passengers were also taken to and from the Soo on Thibert's boat. Joe Andrews, longtime caretaker of the Osborn Preserve near the south end of the island, told me he had ridden on the *Bertha* many times. "It cost 10 cents, one way. Pretty cheap ride." Joe said.

One of my favorite photos among those I turned up during the writing of this book is that of the *Lillie M. H.*

Harry Marks owned some property on Sugar Island adjacent to Duck Lake which was later to become part of the "Osborn Preserve" described in Chapter 5. George Marks, one of Harry's sons, told me that the launch would make about 8 miles per hour, and could be fueled with wood or coal. This boat was probably in use from the turn of the century until the 1920s.

Steam launch **Lillie M.H.** *at Duck Lake ca. 1905. Owner Harry Marks in the bow; note the canopy with luggage on top (courtesy George Marks).*

II. Early Island Economy

Navigation, of course, played an important role throughout the history of the island. Those of us raised in the age of the automobile probably think of an island as being more or less isolated (and it certainly can be, if the ferry can't make its regular runs!) But when the river was the best "highway" in the area, Sugar Island occupied a convenient and key position. It was organized as a township in 1850 according to *Statistics of Michigan*, published in 1870. The only older township in the county is that of Sault Ste. Marie - often listed then as Ste. Marie Township. However, the first reference to Sugar Island Township to be found in the minutes of the Chippewa County Board of Supervisors is dated October 12, 1857. At that time, Philetus Church was the Township Supervisor; shortly thereafter, the County Board of Supervisors consisted of Mr. Church, Mr. Ebenezer Warner, who was supervisor of Ste. Marie Township and Mr. Guy Carleton, who was the County Clerk. (Two's a quorum; three's a crowd!)

Much has been written about Mr. Church, so I will only summarize a few of his accomplishments here. He came to Sugar Island in the late 1840's, establishing himself at the north end of Lake George at the area now known as Churchville Point. That part of the island is very close to Garden River on the Canadian side, which was the site of a Chippewa village. He set up a store or trading post, which must have done a good share of its business with the Garden River Indians when it was first established, as evidenced by the quotation below, from a letter dated November 15, 1850. The letter was written by David Aitken, Indian Sub-Agent at Sault Ste. Marie, Michigan, to William Sprague, Indian Agent at Detroit.

> One of the most thrifty bands we have, living at Garden River, on the Canadian side, do most of their trading with a Gentleman by the name of Church, an American living on the American side, whose trade and intercourse with those Indians has benefitted them much. Mr. Church has never dealt any whiskey or strong drink to them, but has exerted himself ever against it, and the effects are visible amongst those in their very thrifty condition. Would that all traders pursue the same course as Mr. Church in that respect.

Philetus Church eventually ran several businesses at Churchville Point, including a store, a sawmill, a small shipyard and an operation to supply fuel wood to steamboats. The advertisement reproduced here was found in the June 19, 1850 issue of *Lake Superior Journal,* a newspaper which at that time was published in Sault Ste. Marie, Michigan. Since Mr. Church refers to "the past season" in the advertisement, it appears that he had a store operating as early as 1849. Note that he was selling ice, potatoes and other vegetables to passing steamboats. More surprising to me was his offering of ornamental trees. It doesn't seem that there would have been much demand for such trees anywhere in northern Michigan in 1850 - although as indicated, Church was prepared to ship them quite far afield. According to figures cited in the book *River of Destiny* by Milo Quaife and Joseph and Estelle Bayliss, Church sold 3,000 cords of wood to steamboats in 1861, at $1.50 per cord.

WOOD, WOOD.

THE undersigned would call the attention of those interested, to his Large Pile of first quality

STEAM BOAT WOOD.

Which he offers for sale on the most reasonable terms, at his Dock on

SUGAR ISLAND,

Twelve miles below the Saut.. He has a few hundred bushels more of the same sort of Potatoes so much sought for the past season, with which, & a variety of other vegetables boats will be supplied at low prices, to say nothing of the large quantity of Ice always to be found there.

ORNAMENTAL TREES,

Such as the Mountain Ash, Spruce and Fir Trees, will be furnished at short notice. These beautiful trees have been in such demand for several years, that the undersigned will be prepared at any time, to take up and put up with great care these ornamental trees so that they may be safely transported to any distance.

Sugar Island, May 1850.   P. S. CHURCH

Advertisement for items available at P.S. Church's trading post in 1850.

The Quaife and Bayliss book also credits Mr. Church as being the first to cause the channel between the Soo and DeTour in the St. Marys River to be marked. Captain David Tate, master of Church's tug *Pioneer*, set buoys in the spring on his first trip downriver to DeTour, and picked them up on his last run up in the fall. According to an article in *The Evening News*, May 27, 1904, the *Pioneer* was used to place buoys in the Lower St. Marys River from 1865 until 1902.

Mr. Church bought a large amount of land along the river, not all of it on Sugar Island. At one time, he owned the key pieces of land, both on Drummond Island and at DeTour, where the Drummond ferry now docks. He thus had strategic property at the north and south ends of the St. Marys River. He was township supervisor of Sugar Island from 1856 to 1861 and from 1869 to 1880. During several of those years, he was chairman of the Board of Supervisors. He died in 1883 at the age of 71 and is buried in the Maple Ridge Cemetery on the top of Ashmun Hill in Sault Ste. Marie.

Church's Landing from the water, about 1864. The house is the only building that survives *(courtesy Jennylee Church Olesek).*

The oldest photograph reproduced in this book is that of Church's Landing as it looked in 1864; the enlargement shows the house more clearly. The only building remaining in 1991 is the home, designed and built by J. Wells Church in 1862; today, during the summer, very little of the house is visible to passing boats, because of the trees on the property. There is presently a large white pine in the front yard with a diameter of three feet; it may be one of the small trees showing in the photograph. The structure has been listed on the National Register of Historic Places since 1982, due in large measure to the efforts of Roger Pilon. The National Register documentation states that the house is "believed to be a site of outstanding architectural (or archaeological) significance." The Church family sold the property to John and Henry Hickler in 1902. Henry Webster, a Hickler descendant, is the owner at the time of writing of this book, so this property has only been in the hands of two different families since Philetus Church purchased it from the United States in 1849.

Note the piles of wood stacked for sale to steamboats, all of which passed Church's Landing until 1894 (courtesy Jennylee Church Olesek).

The minutes from a meeting of the County Board of Supervisors in 1859 record that "aggregate of the taxable property, real and personal" held in Sugar Island Township in 1859 was $14,000, while the comparable figure for Sault Ste. Marie Township was $100,449. Sugar Island evaluation at that time was thus about fourteen percent of the value of Sault Ste. Marie Township, which included the village of Sault Ste. Marie, so the island was an essential part of the local economy.

Another of the earliest townships to be formed in Chippewa County, not surprisingly, was also on the river - namely, DeTour Township. In its earliest days it was known as "Warner Township," named in honor of Ebenezer Warner, long time supervisor of Sault Ste. Marie Township. First reference to Warner Township in the minutes of the Chippewa County Board of Supervisors occurs in October, 1866, although the township was apparently officially organized in 1850 (the same year Sugar Island was organized,) according to the previously mentioned book, *Statistics of Michigan*. The last reference to Warner is in 1876; the year after, it was changed to DeTour Township. (After 1880 other townships in Chippewa County began to be organized).

In 1876, records indicate that there were 9,698 acres on the tax rolls on Sugar Island, valued at $17,808. Since the area of the island is about 30,000 acres, close to one-third of the land was already on the tax rolls. In Warner Township, the figures were 16,822 acres valued at $38,179, and in Sault Ste. Marie Township, 310,504 acres valued at $658,438. These figures indicate the relative importance that Sugar Island had within the area during that period. Thus, by 1876, the assessed value of Sugar Island had dwindled to about three percent of the value of Sault Ste. Marie Township.

In 1870, *Statistics of Michigan* reported the population of the island as 238, consisting of 48 families. (One hundred years later, the island population was 237). For Sault Ste. Marie Township, the figures were 1,214 people in 223 families. Also counted on the island were 19 horses, 29 "milch cows", 30 "working oxen", 45 other cattle, 40 sheep and 33 swine, for a total value of livestock of $6,146. The comparable value for livestock in Sault Ste. Marie Township was $7,832. A tally of agricultural products sold that year from the island included 1529 pounds of butter, 150 pounds of cheese, 140 gallons of milk, and 40 gallons of wine. We're not told what the wine was made from, but that year, neither wine nor cheese were produced for sale by farmers in

Sault Ste. Marie Township. Island farmers sold 698 tons of hay, compared to 940 tons for Sault Ste. Marie.

Edward Boulley homesteaded land for his farm in the 1880s. The Homestead Act was passed in 1862; the earliest Sugar Island land patented under this act that I found recorded at the Register of Deeds Office was in 1864, by Frank Desmoyer. Other early homesteaders were John Boucha in 1870, Edward Perrault in 1874, and John Tebo, Sophia Edwards and Charles Ware in 1877. Ultimately, about seventy parcels of land on Sugar Island were issued final patents under the Homestead Act after having been "proved up"; the last ones issued were to August Saari in 1917, and Kusti Karpinen in 1920.

Ed Boulley behind his team, Fred and Doll, ca.1920 (courtesy of Ed Pine).

For many years hay was one of the major products of Sugar Island farms. Most of it was brought across the ice between Baie de Wasai and Six Mile Road, and taken to the railroad depot for shipment — much of it to thoroughbred stables in Kentucky, where it was prized. Reeta Freeborn of the Sault recalled seeing load after load pass the Garfield School, where she was both a student and later a teacher. Even after the ferry service was established, travel across the ice was carried on for a time - but by the late thirties such traffic essentially ended.

Several "oldtimers" told me about teams of horses that went through the ice over the years. Albert Currie told me, "Leo DeLisle lost a beautiful team through the ice. Thirteen teams, including Leo's had crossed with loads that morning. It was only an hour later, near lunch time, when Leo headed back for the island with his empty sleigh. He broke through as soon as he got out where the current gets strong, and wears the ice. That was probably the same year the ferry started running (1928)." Leslie Atkins also lost a team, hauling wood between Baie de Wasai and the mainland. He indicated that about five inches of blue ice was considered adequate for a team of horses and a sleigh, as long as the load wasn't too large. They cut holes and measured the ice regularly, but conditions could change pretty fast. If the men thought the ice might be questionable, they sometimes unhitched the sleigh tongue from the harness and pulled the sleigh with a long chain attached to the tongue. This would give a better chance of getting the horses out if they broke through. Sometimes they put a "choker" on the horse, which was a rope around the horse's neck. If the horse broke through, it could get some air into its lungs, but the choker made it difficult to exhale. The horse's lungs would fill up, giving it extra buoyancy, and making it easier to get out of the water. By one account, if a horse went through the ice, and the driver managed to get it out, he would take it to shore and try to get some blankets on it, and pour some whiskey down its throat. Skeptical about this, I asked Jack Fox; his reply was, "I never knew there to be enough whiskey around for the horse to get any."

The forests of the island provided saw-timber, firewood, and, of course, maple syrup. Many families had their sugar-bush to tap in the spring, carrying on a traditional use of the island that was well established when the first white men came to the area. Henry Rowe Schoolcraft described a traditional Chippewa sugaring party in his *History of the Indian Tribes of the U.S.*

Sugaring party at a sugar bush atop the Baie de Wasai Hill, north of Three Mile Road in the late 1920s. Shown are Fred Hatch (kneeling), Louis and Mary Anne Hatch, Alex Atkins, Mary (Hadfield) Murray and her children Babs, Elsie and Josie Hadfield (courtesy Mary Murray).

as a "...sort of carnival." Although it was plenty of work, it was an occasion for a good time, and in Schoolcraft's day, the families sold some of the sugar they made, at 6 cents per pound "payable in merchandise." He said that some families earned as much as $150.00 a season by trading their extra production (I calculated that such an output would require about 10,000 gallons of sap, so it's an impressive figure!) While he doesn't specifically mention Sugar Island, because of its convenient location and abundance of sugar maple trees, it was undoubtedly a well-used area.

Sugar was very important to the traditional Chippewa family. It kept well through the year, was an important source of energy during lean times, and was liberally used as a flavoring, much as some use salt today. Mothers also used it to "help the medicine go down" when they had sick children. (Evidently, before the arrival of traders with iron kettles, the sap was boiled in large bark containers or hollowed out wooden troughs by dropping hot stones in the liquid, according to the article "Indian Origin of Maple Sugar" by H. W. Henshaw.) The importance of maple sugar to the Chippewa is illustrated by the following quotation, taken from the annual report for 1846 filed with the Sault Indian Sub-Agency by the Rev. William H. Brockway, who was the

Sugar Island hardwood about to be taken to the mainland from the Preslan property (courtesy Howard Preslan).

Methodist missionary in charge of the mission school at that time on the mainland side at Little Rapids:

> The school has been kept in regular operation, with the exception of a vacation of about three weeks at the season of sugar making.

Because of the nice stands of hardwood on the island, firewood was taken from there to the mainland for many years. Leslie Atkins had a farm south of the Sault, near Riverside. For quite a few years in the 1920's he purchased wood on the island in the winter and hauled it across the ice for delivery to homes at $2.00 per face cord, "slabbed." Behling Lumber Yard and Consumers Coal purchased wood from Leslie for resale. Leslie told me that his father, Alex, used to say, "You can't sit around all winter and spend what you made in the summer."

A pile of logs at Whipple Point on Lake George, ca. 1930 (courtesy Ed Pine).

George Preslan also hauled a large amount of firewood from the island. He operated a truck farm on the mainland on Gardenville Road, and had several greenhouses for starting plants and raising hothouse tomatoes. He heated the greenhouses with a boiler fired with wood hauled from the island.

A variety of sawmills operated on the island over the years. Already mentioned was the one at Church's Landing, run by Philetus Church. Another was in Payment, run by E.J. Penney. According to Marshall Hunt, this mill closed down sometime just before 1920. When he was a boy, the trestle and tracks were still on the property and the kids in the area used to push the cars uphill a ways and ride them back down. Another sawmill was run by Frank Payment; this steam-powered mill was in the bay on the northwest shore of the island that many refer to now as "Roy's Bay". Waste slabs from the mill can still be seen on the bottom of the bay. Frank's daughter Bernice Maleport indicated that her father was a well-known boatbuilder; he made rowboats, skiffs and small launches from wood he sawed himself. "All the doctors in town had a boat built by Frank Payment," Bernice told me.

Baie de Wasai at the turn of the century is described by Walter Romig as a "three sawmill settlement" in his book *Michigan Place Names,* but I haven't uncovered any documentation of that claim. Perhaps this figure included small, portable sawmills.

There was also a sawmill between about 1900 and 1910 at "Laramie's Corner", which is at the foot of Six Mile Road, on the west side of the island. This mill was run by Ed Pearce. His son Charles Pearce provided me with the following information and photograph.

One of the oxen at the camp had been purchased from the Eagle farm, almost directly across the river. Once, when the flies on the island got bad, the pair of oxen hit the river and started swimming for the mainland. They had to be headed off by boat, and reluctantly went back to the island to face the flies. They were used for general work around the camp, including skidding logs from a log boom (a series of floating timbers chained together in a line, and used to "corral" a large raft of logs, which could then be towed to the mill by a tug). Charlie's caption on the photo of the oxen reads "Tough stew meat!"

Another product that left the island in large amounts was gravel. There wasn't a convenient gravel pit near the river on the mainland south of the Sault so the Sugar Island source was the handiest for roadwork down that way. Some of the island gravel came from the pit behind the county garage on the Baie Hill, while more came from a pit west of the Homestead Road and north of Six Mile Road. It was typically hauled on a sleigh with a box that held about three yards, and was piled up on the mainland side all winter long, for use the next summer. Sometimes, farmers on the mainland side were engaged to haul the gravel where it was needed in the summer, in partial payment of their tax bills. Such piles were made at Five Mile Road and Nine Mile Road.

Ed Pearces' logging camp, near Six Mile Road and West Shore Drive, about 1910 (courtesy Charles Pearce).

Alex Atkins had a contract with the County Road Commission to haul 3000 yards of gravel each winter for three successive years in the late twenties. He employed as many as thirty men with teams, including his son Leslie Atkins, who gave me this information. With a sleigh carrying three to three and one half yards, upwards of 1,000 trips were required, so the traffic across the ice was heavy (in more ways than one!). Two trips per day were typical for each man and his team. The gravel was all loaded by hand at the island pit by six or eight men. When they finished loading one sleigh, there was another waiting to take its place. Leslie recalled that Louis Hatch, Fred Hatch, Bert McKerchie and Jack Piquette were among the men who loaded the sleighs. They must have slept well after a day of loading!

St. Marys River ice made a good travel surface for three or four months of a normal winter; of course ice was also harvested regularly by residents along its shores for use in iceboxes. Allie Rogers recalled that putting up ice for the use of his resort on Lake George was an event that often turned into a good time, with plenty of volunteers ready to pitch in, sharing the good food and drink, as well as the work. In three weekends, they were usually able to put up all the ice needed for his cabins and packing the fish his guests took home.

Around the turn of the century, putting up ice was a major job for some commercial firms in the Sault. One article in a Sault newspaper reported that five firms had put up 6,000 tons of ice for the summer. An article in the Feb. 26, 1891 issue of *The Soo Democrat* lamented the lack of ice in the area as follows:

There is no ice in Lake Superior, which is surprising for this time of year. Captain Emil Endress arrived down from Whitefish Saturday, and he says Lake Superior is clear as a whistle. Even in Whitefish Bay, he says, there is but little ice, and the firm is having trouble filling their icehouses for the season. What ice there is in the bay is thin, and covered with several inches of snow. Talk about summer weather— what is the matter with the Soo when the temperature is not low enough to make good ice? If we do not have more winter weather, we will have to send to the lower peninsula for our summer ice supply.

The island is "blessed" with an abundant supply of stone, and for a time, even that was being sold. Abe Laramie's grandfather, Albert Laramie, homesteaded property in 1881 from Six Mile Road south along the river shoreline and eastward up the hill some still refer to as "Laramie's Hill". When docks were built in those days, they were often constructed using cribs, which are large rectangular "boxes" made out of logs or timbers and filled with stone, and Sugar Island was the source for much of the stone used in this area. Abe's grandfather, father and uncle built a dock 600 feet long, to reach water deep enough for fairly large boats to dock; they put rails on it, built a wagon with flanged wheels, and used it to load stone on boats. All of the loading and unloading was done by hand. Like wood, stone was sold by the cord (a volume four by four by eight feet), and Abe said, "My family sold about 3,000 cords of it, but you'd never know it by looking at the land around there!" (Is it possible that stone is a renewable resource on Sugar Island?)

The land on top of Laramie's Hill didn't have as many stones on it, and for some years the family had about 40 cows, 300 sheep and numerous chickens there. Abe's grandmother made butter, and the job of Abe and his brother was to bring it to the Sault three times a week in a rowboat. They each

Ice harvest in Baie de Wasai, February, 1933. Fred Hatch, and Leo DeLisle are in the picture. Many such operations didn't have a boom such as shown for lifting the ice out of the water, (courtesy Sylvia Hovey).

had a route of regular customers for butter and eggs. "We had two pairs of long oars, but going upriver through the Little Rapids Cut was a job— if you missed one stroke, the boat stopped and started going downriver," Abe told me. (According to the book U.S. Coast Pilot, Little Rapids Cut is the site of the fastest current in the channel portions of the St. Marys River, and the current can reach 2.2 miles per hour there.)

Abe and his brother also had a little "ferry" business for awhile shortly after 1910. They'd row people across the river (much easier, of course, than going upriver to the Soo), and Tate Eagle, a farmer on the mainland near Six Mile Road, would take them to town for two dollars. The Laramie boys had a pole on shore on the mainland side with a large white flag that people could raise to signal that they wanted to cross to the island.

Abe anticipated the Free Trade Agreement between the United States and Canada by about 75 years; wool brought 80 cents a pound in Canada when he was a boy, and only 40 cents a pound in Michigan, so he took the wool from their sheep across the ice on Lake George with a dogsled, to fetch the higher price. He used two dogs to pull the sled, with a third, unharnessed dog ranging out front as a leader which the sled dogs followed. "That worked well, except when a squirrel ran in front of the leader!", he said.

Abe owned a Model T Ford as a young man, and wanted to have it on Sugar Island, even though there were very few roads at the time. He hired a man to haul the car to the island on a scow, but when he wanted it back on the mainland side, he was reluctant to pay the price of hiring the scow again. He began collecting logs to build a raft to transport the car, and his uncle asked him how he intended to get the raft across the river. Abe indicated that he didn't have a plan for that yet, so his uncle told him he would help. The result is shown in the frontispiece drawing of the Model **T** - powered paddle boat. Eventually, Abe crossed the river several times with his "**T**" on the raft, usually drawing salutes and cheers from passing boats. He stood behind the car, steering with an oar placed in a "crotch."

III. Ferries and Roads

The first regularly scheduled ferry to bring cars to the island was the *Service*. It began operating July 1, 1928; an entry in *The Evening News* on July 3, 1928 states:

> The Sugar Island ferry, operated by Elmo Kibby, began operations Sunday when 30 automobiles were carried from the island to the mainland.
>
> While all graveling on the Island approach has not been completed, the road was in good condition and the automobiles had no difficulty.
>
> ....When business warrants, a big scow will be used to supplement the boat.
>
> The ferry is operating from 7 A.M. to 10 P.M. and crosses from the mainland and island whenever there is a call.
>
> Ferry rates for automobiles varies from 45 cents for light cars to 75 cents for heavy trucks. Foot passenger fare is 15 cents.

In addition to cars and trucks, the ferry carried horse-drawn wagons during this period; the wagon had to be backed onto the ferry, the team unhitched and put alongside. Marie Maleport told me that the ferry rate for a car was based on its length, and her father-in-law, Adelore Maleport, had a Buick that was long enough to put it into the next higher fare category than most cars. He found that if he took both bumpers off, the car qualified for the lower rate— so Adelore's Buick was bumperless from then on!

The *Service*, according to records cited by Fr. Edward J. Dowling, was 51 feet 8 inches long and had a displacement of 16 tons. It was a converted wooden-hulled launch. Although a ferry service had been opposed by some islanders, that first day of operation must have been an exciting one.

For a short while prior to 1928, the *Service* landed with vehicles at Brassar Point, rather than at the present causeway, according to several older islanders. Pete Causley said that it used to be necessary to drive through a stretch of shallow water and up some planks to get on or off the boat on the island side.

The Service, the first regularly scheduled ferry for automobiles, run by Elmo Kibby, ca. 1930, note the "K" on pennant (courtesy Emery and Donna Corbiere).

"We carried some rags so we could dry off the distributor and wires when we used that landing. And we had to back the car up that steep hill at Brassar, because there wasn't any fuel pump on that car— gasoline was gravity-fed— and going uphill in reverse kept the tank above the motor!", Pete said. The deckhand sometimes stood on one end of the plank as a car started off the boat. Later, a good dock was built at Brassar Point to handle cars.

The *Service* was used until 1932, at which time it was condemned as unsafe (apparently by the Marine Navigation and Inspection Bureau) and was replaced by the *Beaver*, which was built in the Soo for E.E. Peterman and Sons. This ferry could carry four or five cars; note the hump in the middle of the deck, which was necessary to make room for the engine. One of the pilots of that era was Frank Smith — known to many as "Pike-Pole" Smith. He sometimes ran the ferry without a deckhand, bringing the boat in to the dock, then hustling out of the pilothouse and using a pike-pole to nudge it into position to be tied up.

The Beaver, the second of the ferries, ca. 1930s *(courtesy John Wellington)*.

Even after regular ferry service began, the boat didn't necessarily run all winter. That apparently depended on the severity of the winter. As noted in the reference at the end of the chapter, the ferry was laid up for a portion of the winter of 1938. Reg Fox told me that he, Jimmy Stevens, Herb Palmer, George Adams, Dan Boyer and Tauno Ruona sawed the ferry free from ice one April, so that it could start running again. The job took about six hours.

The *Beaver* ran until 1937, when Peterman's second ferry was placed in service. This vessel was simply named *Scow No. 1.* When it was rebuilt in 1944, it was given the more distinctive name *Chippewa*. For a time while the *Chippewa* was being rebuilt, the *Beaver* was used for the ferry runs. But it too failed a Marine Navigation Bureau inspection and the inspectors refused to grant a waiver, with the result that ferry service was curtailed for about two weeks. The vessel *Robert A.*, owned by Henry Thibert of Neebish Island, was used between May 5 and August 7 of 1944, at which time the rebuilt *Chippewa* came back on line. After these modifications, the *Chippewa* had a displacement of 26 tons.

The **Chippewa***, the third of ferries, ca. 1940s (courtesy John Wellington).*

Some of the equipment from the *Beaver* was used in rebuilding the *Chippewa,* and afterward the hull of the *Beaver* was sold for use as an unpowered scow to the Sturgeon Bay Co of Cleveland, Ohio.

The* Sugar Islander *as it was originally built, ca. 1950s. Of interest to local hamburger lovers is the original Clyde's Drive-In in the background *(courtesy John Wellington).*

The Chippewa County Road Commission acquired the ferry operation from Mr. Peterman in 1945, and at that time the island residents asked the Commission to appropriate money to build a larger, steel ferry. In 1947, the *Sugar Islander* was built by the Lock City Machine and Marine Company in Sault Ste. Marie for the County Road Commission. The vessel carried nine cars, and had a displacement of 67 tons. The pilot house was at deck level originally, as shown in the photograph.

The County Road Commission sold the ferry and gave a franchise for its operation to Kenneth Bonathan in 1948. Bonathan acquired the *Chippewa* as well; he sold the engine from it to Fred Cardinal, who was building a ferry for Neebish Island at the time. The unpowered *Chippewa* was subsequently used as a barge to service Lime Island, according to John Wellington.

Some time during the fifties, the pilot house of the *Sugar Islander* was placed on a superstructure, leaving more room on the deck to accommodate cars that were becoming wider. Bonathan sold the ferry operation to John and Jim Wellington in 1961. In 1971, the Soo Drydock Company modified the ferry significantly for Wellington Transportation Co. The ferry was cut in two and lengthened by inserting a twenty foot section, and the deck was widened by 18 inches on each side. This increased the capacity of the ferry from nine to twelve cars. (The boat may have as many as sixteen cars on it presently, but that is because cars are smaller than they were in the early seventies). The hull was modified in 1972 because of mounting problems with ice in the ferry lanes, caused by winter navigation. Each end of the boat was lengthened by about twenty inches, while being reshaped to ride up on the ice better, and was strengthened in general. She was also repowered from 200 horsepower to 550 horsepower at that time.

Wellington Transportation sold the operation to Poirier Marine in 1973, and Poirier ran it until it was purchased by the Eastern Upper Peninsula Transportation Authority in 1979. In the fiscal year 1989-90 the ferry carried 173,854 vehicles and 310,150 passengers, with about 65% of the annual traffic coming from "regular" users (those who purchase books of tickets) and 35% from tourists and other visitors. The ferry made 34,735 crossings that year.

Until E.U.P.T.A took over, the County Road Commission was responsible for building and maintaining the docks on both sides of the river. The

Sugar Islander attempting to reach dock on the mainland side, January, 1972. Coast Guard cutter Naugatuck was assisting (courtesy John Wellington).

original contract for the docks was awarded to Great Lakes Dredge and Dock Co. The causeway was apparently constructed by adding to the dike which had been built in 1893 when dredging in Little Rapids was being done. Until sometime in the late fifties or early sixties, there were three wooden bridges on the causeway --- one of which was an arched bridge across "the 8 foot channel," to allow small boats to pass underneath, saving a roundabout trip if it was desired to go from one side of the causeway to the other. (The low bridge nearest the ferry used to be a pretty good place to fish for walleyes, and the high bridge was an exciting place to swim, because you could jump from a good height into fast water and get quite a ride).

Construction of the causeway, showing pilings of one of the bridges orginally there, ca. spring 1928 (courtesy of Chippewa County Road Commission).

During World War II, the U.S. Army had some anti-aircraft gun emplacements and searchlights placed where the Hilltop Bar now is. (Some say barrage-balloons as well, but there is disagreement on this). Upwards of 50 men were stationed there. They didn't have cooking facilities, so they were supplied food from Fort Brady. Together with other needs, this amounted to fairly steady traffic on the ferry and causeway. In 1943, when the wooden bridges were in need of repair, Louis Levin, the Chippewa County Road Engineer at the time, reasoned that the military might be willing to provide some assistance with the repairs. The correspondence file on island matters at the Road Commission office contains a letter Levin wrote to Col. Becthold at Fort Brady in which he requested such assistance. I didn't find any reply that might have been received.

The causeway on Sugar Island, looking towards the ferrydock, ca. 1950 (courtesy Chippewa County Road Commission).

Levin approached the military at least one other time for help with island transportation. As World War II was winding down, he wrote several letters to agencies in Washington hoping to locate a surplus landing craft which might be useable as a backup to the ferries at Sugar, Neebish, and Drummond Island in case of breakdowns. This time a reply was received, as described in the accompanying article.

Levin Can't Get Battleship for St. Mary's River Service

10-13-45

All he asks for is to buy LST, LSI to convert into ferry.

Right back where he started from is County Engineer Louis F. Levin, who has written repeatedly to War Shipping Administration, Assistant Deputy Administrator for Small Vessels, Commodore Edmond J. Moran, U. S. N. R., Department of Commerce Building, Washington 25, D. C. for information as to where he can get a boat— any boat—to pinch hit when one of the three ferries maintained by the county goes "on the blink."

Finally, in desperation, Levin wrote to Secretary of the Navy Forrestal himself, who referred him to —War Shipping Adiminstration, Assistant Deputy Administrator for Small Vessels, etc.

Levin was further informed that under no circumstances may he purchase a battleship, aircraft carrier, cruiser, destroyer or submarine to carry passengers between Sugar Island, Neebish Island or Drummond Island and the mainland.

The U. S. Maritime Commission— War Shipping Administration has been delegated the authority to sell in accordance with the provisions of Surplus Property Act of 1944, Surplus Property Board Regulation No. 1, Order 1, all vessels except the above named.

So Levin, who doesn't want a battleship or a submarine, is just sitting tight. Something may come of it after all. Meanwhile, for want of a vital part which is on its way, the Sugar Island ferry is temporarily out of operation.

County engineer denied surplus submarine for ferry service, Evening News article, October 13, 1945.

Prior to regular ferry service, some cars were taken to the island on an individual basis by Elmo Kibby, some were probably brought there on a variety of scows, and some undoubtedly crossed the ice in the winter. A map from 1931 at the Chippewa County Road Commission office is partially reproduced on the next page to show the roads at that time. There were 12 miles of road on the island that were the responsibility of the county, while the remainder of the roads were maintained by the township. Some existing roads are conspicuously absent, of course, as they had not yet been built. Others that are shown on the map are no longer open. In 1931, there was a total of 67 miles of road on the island, which is exactly the total for 1991. About four miles of this total are considered "seasonal road," and are not kept plowed in the winter months.

The names of the roads that I have shown did not come from the road commission map; they were taken from a Corps of Engineers marine map published in 1898. Note that the Brassar Road originally was the east-west road through Brassar, while the north-south road through that settlement was known as McMahon Road, after Charles McMahon. Two other early families, the LaCoys and Gravels, had roads named after them as well.

In 1931-1932, the Michigan State Legislature passed the McNitt Act, which required counties to assume, over the subsequent four year period, responsibility for all roads then being maintained by the various townships. Thus by 1936, all roads on the island had been taken over by the county.

As late as 1937, snow plowing on the island was handled by horse-drawn plows. Men and their teams were hired when it was necessary, and one of the men who drove a team on the "Homestead run" was Jack Fox. He told me:

> The roads were plowed with a V-plow, and the banks were rolled with a big roller. We used three or four teams on the plow, and four or five teams on the roller. I was just a kid when I went on that freeze-to-death outfit. You made nine dollars a day, man and team. We had to be at McIntosh Corner (the corner of Three Mile Road and Homestead Road) at 6 A.M. ready to go. That run to Homestead took about twelve hours, there and back. Then when you got back, you had maybe four miles to go to get home, and they didn't pay you for that. And in the spring of the

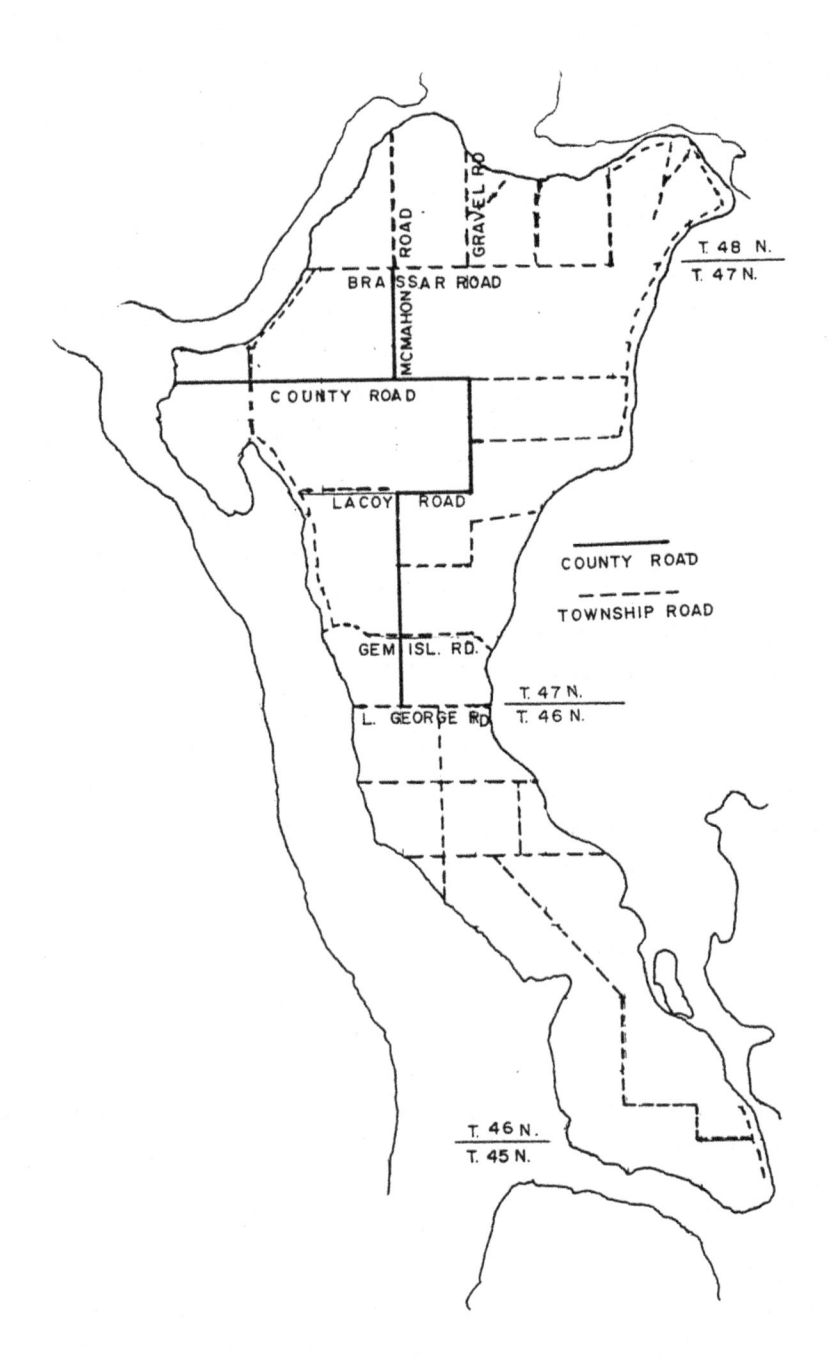

Map showing roads on Sugar Island in 1931.

year for about three weeks the fields would be bare and the roadway would be built up about two feet above the fields.

The roads and ferry service were the topic of several articles that appeared in the school newspaper published at the Baie de Wasai School during the 1937-38 school year. One such article, in the February, 1938 issue, entitled "More About the Roads" stated in part:

A man who is supposed to be matured mentally and has had considerable number of years of experience in the construction of roads and the removal of snow from the highways is trying to make the Sugar Island people believe that a powered plow could not be used satisfactorily on our roads.... Our roads are in as bad a shape during the winter months as the worn and torn roads in France during the World War, judging from the pictures I have seen in my father's regimental history.

Horse-drawn snow roller, used to roll down the snow banks after plowing (courtesy Chippewa County Road Commission).

It is not enough that the roads are impassable, but now we are deprived of ferry service. The mailman crosses at the head of the island, and every minute he is in peril of his life. Must someone actually drown there before the seriousness of our situation is acknowledged by those who are able to remedy it? Is it not enough that so many farmers have lost horses by drowning because the crossing is always so unsafe in the winter when the ferry quits running?

The ferry was kept running all of the winter '35 and '36. Are our winters getting colder now?

Let's do away with these inconveniences. Make your slogan: "Good roads and better ferry service for Sugar Island."

IV. The Island People

Early records of the population of Sugar Island are understandably quite sketchy. U.S. Census records of Chippewa County are available at the Bayliss Library on microfilm from 1830 until 1910 (72 years must pass before detailed census information is made public), but until the island became a township, Sugar Island residents are not listed separately— thus it isn't possible from census records to determine accurately who lived there until 1860. Incidentally, as late as 1850 there were still quite a few men in the Sault area who gave their occupation as "voyageur" to the census taker.

Records maintained in the office of the Chippewa County Register of Deeds allow for determination of the ownership of island land; the earliest recorded purchases were made from the United States in the late 1840's, but it is likely that many who owned land on the island didn't actually live there.

Native Americans were, of course, the first to make the island their home, and their descendants have made up a significant portion of the population up to the present day. Henry Schoolcraft gives a census of the Native American population on the "St. Mary's River, American side" in 1830 as totaling 275 "full-blood" and 161 "mixed blood." He mentions Sugar Island as one of the population centers, but doesn't break the population down. He gives the total population of the Sault Ste. Marie area as 918 in 1830, so almost half of the residents in the area at that time were at least partly of Native American descent.

The Treaty of Fond du Lac was signed in 1826 between the United States and the Chippewa Tribe. This treaty contained a provision for the tribe to make a grant of land to various Chippewa and "half-breed" families in this region. A portion of Article IV of that treaty reads

> ...the Chippewa tribe... grant to each of the persons described in the schedule hereunto annexed... six hundred and forty acres of land, to be located, under the direction of the President of the United States, upon the islands and shore of the St. Mary's river, wherever good land enough for this purpose can be found... The locations for Oshauguscodaywayqua and her descendants shall be adjoining the lower part of the military

reservation (Fort Brady), and upon the head of Sugar Island. The persons to whom grants are made shall not have the privilege of conveying the same, without the permission of the President.

Oshauguscodaywayqua was the wife of John Johnston, fur trader and one of the most prominent figures in Sault Ste. Marie history. As indicated, Mrs. Johnston and each of her children and grandchildren were to receive a section (one square mile) of land. Forty-five individuals or heads of families are listed in the schedule appended to the treaty which itemized recipients of the land, but it was only the Johnston family land whose location was specifically described. Some books indicate that Sugar Island was singled out for Mrs. Johnston in order to provide a "sugarbush" for her, which certainly seems plausible. Despite having spent a good deal of time trying to locate records which would indicate exactly what piece of land Mrs. Johnston selected on the island, I have been unable to do so.

The Treaty of Washington was signed in 1836, one of the chief negotiators having been Henry Schoolcraft. In this treaty, the Chippewa, Ottawa, and Potawatomi tribes agreed to cede most of the Upper Peninsula, including Sugar Island, and a large piece of the Lower Peninsula, to the United States. The treaty provided, however, that certain tracts of land be reserved for use of members of the three tribes for a period of five years, as noted in the quotation below:

ARTICLE THIRD. There shall also be reserved for the Chippewas living north of the straits of Michilimackinac, the following tracts for the term of five years from the date of the ratification of this treaty, and no longer, unless the United States shall grant them permission to remain on said lands for a longer period, that is to say: Two tracts of three miles square each, on the north shores of said straits, between Pointe-au-Barbe and Millecoquin River, including the fishing grounds in front of such reservations, to be located by a council of the chiefs.
The Beaver Islands ... Round island, opposite Michilimackinac .... The islands of the Chenos (Les Cheneaux, evidently) ... Sugar island, with its islets, in the river of St. Mary's ... [and several other tracts, near Point

Iroquois, the Tahquamenon River, Grand Island, and Green Bay].

Sometime prior to the signing of this treaty, apparently Sugar Island and the other tracts of land mentioned above had been designated as permanent reservations, since later in the treaty occurs the following:

The sum of two hundred thousand dollars (shall be paid to the Chippewa and Ottawa tribes), in consideration of changing the permanent reservations in article two and three to reservations for five years only.

It is also clear from the treaty that an effort was to be made to relocate the Chippewas and Ottawas to western lands:

ARTICLE EIGHTH. It is agreed, that as soon as the said Indians desire it, a deputation shall be sent to the southwest of the Missouri River, there to select a suitable place for the final settlement of said Indians, which country, so selected and of reasonable extent, the United States will forever guaranty and secure to said Indians.

The Treaty of 1855, negotiated at Detroit, reserved about 40 sections of land in the Sault Ste. Marie area "for Indian purposes". Among those sections reserved were the following on Sugar Island: sections 2,3,4,11,14,and 15 of Township 47N, R2E and section 34 of Township 48N, R2E. (Several of these are partial sections on the shore). Records at the Register of Deeds Office indicate that in the 1860's and 1870's, some of that land was selected by Native American families, pursuant to the terms of the treaty.

The earliest white settler on the island, by several accounts, was Michael Payment, who evidently settled there in the late 1840's. He purchased land in the area now called Payment in 1848, according to records in the Register of Deeds office. Philetus Church purchased land in the area that was to become Churchville Point in 1849, and settled there soon afterward, so two of the earliest families left their mark on the island maps.

The 1860 census shows a total of 240 people calling Sugar Island their home. Six families with the name Payment are listed — the heads of household being Philbert, Michael, Moses, Alexis, Alfred and Joseph. Michael,

Alfred, Moses and Joseph were brothers, and Philbert was Joseph's son. They were all born at or near Rigaud, Quebec, according to information contained in an extensive genealogy of the Payment family written in 1987 by Susan Payment. It seems likely that Alexis was also a relative, but he was not listed in the genealogy. The six families totaled 33 individuals, thus accounting for 14 percent of the island's population at that time! Five of the Payment men gave their occupation as farmer, and Joseph was a shoemaker.

Francis Xavier Payment, nephew of Michael, Alfred, Moses and Joseph, joined his uncles and their families on Sugar Island sometime between 1860 and 1869, because he was married on the island in the latter year. He was a carpenter and skilled boat-builder and for many years he had a shop in the Sault where he built boats. According to an entry in one of J. Wells Church's diaries, Francis X. Payment was the man who built the motor boat Clyde, pictured in Chapter One. His wife Harriet ran a boarding house for men who worked at the Union Carbide plant.

Francis Xavier Payment and wife Harriet, outside of their boarding house in Sault Ste. Marie, ca. 1915 (courtesy Mary MacMaster).

Some of the other family names on the census of 1860 are: Wilson, Palmer, Laisk (Leask), Gravelle, Sewbiston (Sebastian), Levoines, Day, and Parault (Perrault). I tallied the birthplaces of the heads of household to see where these early islanders came from. Two were from Scotland, three from England, five from New York, twenty-three from Canada, and nineteen from Michigan. Most if not all of the Michigan-born were Native American. The Palmer name survives on current island maps as Palmer Point, on the north end of the island. William Palmer purchased land including the point in 1848; he subsequently sold it to P. S. Church.

By 1880, the population had grown to 544. Although the most common listed occupation was again that of farmer, by this time several of the men are shown as being sawyers, wood choppers, and sawmill workers. A couple of boat-builders, light-house keepers, and a wood-merchant, Allen Rains, also appear. (No butcher, no baker, nor candlestick maker!)

This census also listed the birthplaces of the parents of the individuals shown and the preponderance of Canadian heritage is immediately clear. (Between 1871 and 1881, 400,000 Canadians emigrated to the United States, which represented 10% of Canada's population at that time!) A large percentage of the Canadian immigrants were French-Canadian. The names Boucher, Masta, Brassar, Myotte (Mailhot), Thibert, Thibodeau, Perrault, DeLisle, Laramie and DeLorme are some of the French family names found on the 1880 census. The Brassar name is also part of island geography now; it evidently is a corruption of the name Bourassa, which is how it appears in the earliest records of land transactions. (Bourassa is a common name in Quebec - there are 370 Bourassa entries in a recent Montreal telephone book).

Incidentally, Jesse Wells Church, son of Philetus Church, was the census-taker on Sugar Island in 1880. The records were all kept in longhand, and I would add to the list of his many talents that of writing in a beautiful, artistic hand. He attended the University of Michigan and later graduated from medical school; in 1868, he moved to Harbor Island, just off Drummond Island where he lived for many years with his family, practicing medicine and finding time to design and build boats as he became one of the area's leading citizens. (The census taker in 1980 probably also writes in a nice hand, but the main reason she was given Sugar Island as her area was that she owned a four-wheel drive vehicle to negotiate the roads in April!)

Allen Rains

Two of the families that came to Sugar Island from Canada in the 1870's were those of Allen and Norman Rains. They have already been mentioned in Chapter One in connection with the lighter ship *St. Mary*, which they built in 1875 and operated for about eight years. The brothers were among the twenty-five children of Major William Kingdom Rains, who settled on St. Joseph's Island in the 1830's. They purchased about 260 acres of land at the very southern tip of Sugar Island in the area now known as Harwood Point. The quotation below, concerning Allen Rains, was taken from material written by Jim Rains of Hemlock, N.Y., for distribution at a family reunion for Rains descendants in 1990. Jim is a grandson of Allen Rains, and the material is quoted with his permission:

Around 1877, Allen purchased what is substantially the entire south end of Sugar Island. With the help of his two juvenile sons, and some Indian friends, he (Allen) built an absolutely beautiful home. It was called Midriver, and was located on the main shipping channel to and from Sault Ste. Marie. A huge dock with a T-shaped platform at the far end was constructed for the use of mailboats and freighters. There was ample room for the storage of the birch-log fuel that the steamboats of the day needed in great quantities. Allen sold a lot of it. In addition, he was at the same time in the civil service employ of the United States Post Office and the U.S. Lighthouse Service, as well as being county game warden. I can attest to the fact that he really worked at the lighthouse job. Tending the main channel up-range lights, as well as the danger ranges on Hen-and-Chicken Islands and in Sam Fields' meadow on Neebish Island required a lot of rowing. I know. I've done it. And his work for the Post Office required that he deliver all mail from his dock at Midriver to the Post Office at Homestead — by wheelbarrow! This I have also done, though I must admit that there wasn't too much mail, as a general thing. Never more than fifty or sixty pounds, in one or two pouches. But it had to be done. All in addition to running a large farm, vegetable garden, strawberry patch, sheep herd, dairy cows, icehouse. And in the spring, he made and sold large quantities of maple syrup. In all, he kept busy.

For a short while, there apparently was an exception to Jim's statement about the weight of the mail. The following anecdote is taken from a privately published book written in 1971 by Helen Seymour Wiley. Mrs. Wiley's book is about the Wiley cabin, built about 1920, just north of the original Rains property:

> One summer, a woman from Chicago, vacationing in one of the Nelson cottages, collected rocks for a fireplace and shipped some in a carton almost daily. Allen Rains, lean, fiery and crotchety, swore so lustily at the weight and number of these packages that Mrs. Nelson trembled lest he dump her U.S. mail into the bushes.

Allen Rains' original dock was located almost a mile north of the southern tip of Sugar Island on the old channel running up the east side of the island. By 1894, with the opening of the Hay Lake Channel, this was no longer the main route. Sometime before 1898, a new dock was built at the southernmost tip of the island which was ideally located for servicing boats using the new channel. Both docks are shown on a chart from 1898; the earlier one is called "Rains Dock", and the one on the new channel is called "Rains Dock (New)". In 1900, Mr. Rains sold a portion of the property where the old dock was located to the United States. The U. S. Lighthouse Service took over the property and ran it as a buoy station. Rains sold more of his frontage on the east channel to the United States in 1907.

Allen Rains was Township Supervisor of Sugar Island from 1891 through 1895, and from 1897 through 1899. He died in 1932 at the age of 91.

The 1910 census gives a figure of 121 Native Americans living on Sugar Island in 26 family units. (The census records for that period kept Native Americans on a separate roll.) For the same year, there were 494 "Non-Indian" people, in 97 family units. Familiar island names such as Gurnoe, Hatch, Boulley, Cadreau, Edwards, Mendoskin, LaCoy, Shawano and Andrews are among the families listed on the "Indian Census Roll". Some of these families were, of course, of mixed ancestry.

Mary (Hatch) Murray

One of the most informative sources of personal recollections used in this book has been Mary (Hatch) Murray. Mary's father, Louis Hatch, was born in 1855 on an island in the Soo Rapids.

Mary (Boulley) Pine, splitting ash strip for a basket, ca. 1914 (courtesy Ed Pine).

The island no longer exists; it was removed, probably about 1880, when the locks were enlarged. Her mother, Mary Anne Perrault, was born in Payment in 1862 where she was baptized by Bishop Frederic Baraga. Mary herself was born in a log cabin at Baie de Wasai in 1903, and grew up there. Ojibwa was the language of her family. Her father earned a living by fishing, cutting wood, loading gravel onto sleighs in the winter, and for many years was caretaker of several cottages on Steere's Island (near Rotary Park at the Soo; all but one of the cottages are gone now). He served as "moderator" of the Baie de Wasai school for 27 years, meaning that he was in charge of the school district's money. Mary told me, "He couldn't read or write, but he was moderator for 27 years. Now beat that! Of course, in those days, they didn't know anything about credit; if they wanted anything, and there wasn't enough money, they didn't get it."

Certificate of Baptism

†

Holy Name of Mary Church
Sault Sainte Marie, Mich.

:–: This is to Certify :–:

That _Mary Anne Perrault_
Child of _Joseph Perrault_
and _Angelique Kijiashinohwe_
born in _Sugar Island, Mich._
on the _19th_ day of _September 1862_
was **Baptized**
on the _29th_ day of _September 1862_
According to the Rite of the Roman Catholic Church
by the Most Rev. Bishop Frederick Baraga
the Sponsors being Jean Baptiste Johweijanta
Catherine Perrault
as appears from the Baptismal Register of this Church.
Dated _this 24th February 1941_
Father Paul Prud'homme

Certification of the baptism of Mary Anne (Perrault) Hatch by Bishop Frederic Baraga (courtesy of Mary (Hatch) Murray).

Mary Murray and her uncle, Dan Perrault, ca. 1916 (courtesy of Mary (Hatch) Murray).

Mary Murray, ca.1985 (courtesy Mary Murray, photo by Preston Hogue).

Mary has a strong sense of her Native American heritage, and has been working towards the establishment of a "Museum of Many Fires," signifying the fact that traditionally many different tribes used the area near the Soo Rapids. She appeared before a committee of the United States Senate in about 1975, helping to raise funds for the Sault Tribe. She has a memory like a steel trap, and is also a person who saves things. (For example, a sample ballot for the Township of Sugar Island election held April 5, 1937). I came to cherish both qualities while working on this book.

I discovered a photograph in a collection known as the Gordon Daun Collection in the Steere Room at Bayliss Public Library in Sault Ste. Marie. Mr. Daun had written above the photograph the title:

Chief Wa-ba-keke of Sugar Island. A true representative of the Chippewa race. Prize winning photograph taken by W.J. Bell.

The photograph was probably taken about 1890. I asked Mary Murray if she knew anything about Chief Wa-ba-keke; she said she had heard her parents speak of him and his family, but he probably had died before she was born. Chief Wa-ba-keke's name is among those listed on the 1870 Annuity Roll showing names of Native Americans who received annuity payments from the United States government. A death certificate is on file at the Chippewa County Clerk's Office for a man named Joseph Wahbagayke from Sugar Island; he died in 1903 at the age of 97, and this may be the man pictured below. It is indeed a striking photograph, and I would like to be able to add more about him. Unfortunately, I am aware of nothing more that is known about him.

Chief Waba-keke's photograph, as well as those in Chapter One depicting the wreck of the *Susan E. Peck* and the dredging of the Hay Lake channel were all taken by photographer W.J. Bell. William J. Bell came to Sault Ste. Marie from Barrie, Ontario, sometime prior to 1890. He operated a photography studio in the Sault for almost fifty years. Many of the photographs which document the history of the area are his, so we are indebted to him for preserving a visual record of our heritage. Mr. Bell died in 1940.

Chief Wa-ba-kake (White Hawk) ca. 1890s, by W. J. Bell (courtesy of Bayliss Public Library).

Alfred Leask

"Alfie" Leask was a well-known figure on Sugar Island for many years. He died in June, 1987, two months short of his 101st birthday. He literally spent most of his life on the river; his mother was cook on a tugboat, and Alfie was born on it somewhere off DeTour. He was a crane operator on river projects as a young man, and did a lot of "hardhat" diving on the lakes and the eastern seaboard. If a vessel was "holed" below the water line in this area, Alfie was often called in to make temporary repairs. He was also called numerous times to recover the body of a drowning victim. Gordon Church, a grandson of J. Wells Church, was a tender for Alfie for a time - that is, the man who stayed on the boat and looked after the air supply to the diver, and communicated with him by tugging on the lines. Gordon described his work with Alfie to me:

> Alfie didn't care who the tender was, he'd still dive. Another diver on one of our jobs would only go down if his brother was the tender. Alfie had me put a few drops of fish oil in the compressor line when he went down, because he said it helped him breathe better. The next diver to use the suit usually put the helmet in the water and ran air through it for ten minutes before he'd consider putting it on, because of that fishy smell!

Alfie Leask, ca. 1910 (courtesy Rose Menard).

Alfie was forced to quit diving at the age of 72, when the insurance company his employer dealt with refused to insure him any longer. In all the years working on and under the water, he never learned how to swim.

Obviously not a man to let his age stop him, Alfie began building some dredging equipment in his late seventies, putting a crane on a scow he built. Thinking more like a 30 year old, his dream was to dredge a boat channel and harbor in the bay near his home on the northwest side of the island, and then put up some cabins to rent. The dredge is still in the bay, where it has been for 20 odd years. Chum Menard, Alfie's nephew, told me about a time he stopped in to see his uncle; Alfie was about ninety- five at the time, and had been puttering around with some projects before Chum arrived. He said to Chum, "I can't understand it. I do a few things around here now, and I'm all out of gas!"

On good authority, I've been told that the night Alfie died, the boom on his crane crashed to the deck of the scow.

Alfie Leask at Senior Citizen dinner at the Community Center on Sugar Island, ca. 1985 (photograph by Mary L Adams).

The Finnish

Early in the book I mentioned three names by which Sugar Island has been known. I could have listed a fourth - Sokeri Saari, which is Finnish for Sugar Island.

I remember as a young boy being fascinated by the accents of the Finnish people my parents knew. That was probably my first direct connection with the larger world we live in. (My dad seemed partial to cursing in Finnish when he did something like hitting his thumb with a hammer. Inevitably, some English words, rolling off tongues that grew up in Finnish, were worth remembering. As when a fellow who was working on his well went to the Baie store and asked if they had one of those "sex valves" - meaning a check valve.) I guess I always assumed that this ethnic group had been part of the island mix of people almost since "day one." In fact, the early Finnish settlers arrived on Sugar Island during the WWI era and the 1920s. (Tax records for 1916 show no names of Sugar Island landowners that were obviously Finnish; in 1931, the same records showed about 55 names that appeared to be Finnish, out of about 500 recorded as owning land on Sugar Island). Most of the families apparently did not come directly from Finland, coming instead by way of such places as the western U.P., lower Michigan, the Chicago area, and Canada. The immigration of Finns to Drummond Island occurred ten or fifteen years earlier, led by an interesting woman named Maggie Walz. That story, and much more is to be found in the book *Islands of the Manitou* by Kathryn Belden Ashley.

One of the first Finns to arrive on Sugar Island was Frank Aaltonen, who was Township Supervisor in 1921, 1922, 1926, and 1927. Mr. Aaltonen was active in promoting the island among fellow Finns. He evidently acted as a broker or intermediary in a significant number of land transactions in which Finnish families acquired land on the island, and promoted it among Finnish settlers in the western Upper Peninsula and Wisconsin. He also bought and sold a good deal of land in his own right between 1916 and 1928. He is given credit by some for being a major force behind getting the causeway improved and the ferry dock built, so that ferry service would be possible— and that view is supported by records in the county road commission office which indicate Aaltonen led a delegation of islanders before the commission several times regarding establishment of ferry service. Aaltonen and his family left Sugar Island about 1928, moving to Massachusetts.

Oscar Maki brought his family to the island in 1920. Sylvia (Maki) Hovey remembers, as a girl of nine, the family and their furniture being brought to Brassar Point on a scow by Elmo Kibby. Her father had worked in lumber camps in Ontario for several years, and Sylvia was born in Wawa, Ontario. She started school in Sault, Ontario, "fresh from the lumber camps," having spoken nothing but Finnish. Mr. Maki acquired farmland on the road to Hay Point in 1920 and established a prosperous farm there. During World War II, he raised "fields and fields" of flax. He also ran a sawmill for a time, cutting railroad ties during the war, and sawlogs for the Escanaba Veneer Mill. Sylvia recalled:

> Dad worked a long day then, because he had to care for the cows in the morning, then head for the woods to work with his crew all day, while mother separated the cream back at the farm.

Sylvia (Maki) Hovey, 1991, with traditional Finnish skis, made by Lauri Karimo (photograph by author).

Sylvia's sister, Impi (Maki) Curlis, taught school for a number of years in the Soo area, many of them on Sugar Island.

Frank Vuori's family also came to the island in 1920, from Wisconsin. Mr. Vuori had had a farm there, and his son Alex recalls that his father was able to buy 200 acres of land on Sugar Island for the same amount that he had sold his 40 acre farm for in Wisconsin. Frank Aaltonen was an agent in the sale, since Mr. Vuori spoke only Finnish. Mr. Kibby brought the family by boat to Baie de Wasai; there was a trail going from the Baie up through the woods to the hill on which the farm sat, which would be a distance of less than a mile. Since the present road from the Baie Church to the ferry road did not exist, getting the family belongings to the farm by horse and wagon involved a more roundabout trip of about six miles. Alex and his sister Sally spoke only Finnish when they started school at Baie de Wasai.

In 1921, John and Milja Keko and their daughters Gwen and Paula came to Sugar Island from Waukegan, Illinois, arriving at William Walker's Landing at Nine Mile Point. John Keko had purchased over two hundred acres of land fronting on Lake George from Frank Aaltonen, sight unseen. While his wife and daughters stayed with the Aaltonen family, John went to his property and cleared the rocks and trees from enough of the land to make room for a home and the mandatory sauna which he built. Their story is perhaps representative of the experience of many who carved a place for themselves on Sugar Island, whether Finnish or not, and I will let Bill and Nancy (Kauppi) Saunders continue it. Nancy is the daughter of Gwen (Keko) Kauppi, and granddaughter of John and Milja:

> The Keko family faced many hardships those first years. They were truly twentieth century pioneers. Land had to be cleared of trees, by hand. Once the trees were gone, the land was obscured by thousands upon thousands of rocks that had to be moved. Smaller ones were simply picked up while larger ones had to be split into more manageable pieces by sledge or heating and quenching. Most found their way into rock fences surrounding the Keko home and adjacent fields. Tools, additional furniture and a barn needed to be built. Some of the necessary tools were constructed on the kitchen floor of Keko's new home. All of these things to do at once, but none produced income. In the meantime, money was needed to buy the things that couldn't be made on the kitchen floor, not to mention the basic food and clothing needs of a

young family. So, after only a short time on Sugar Island, the following winter John left Milja and the two girls behind while he traveled to Detroit to find employment. Imagine, leaving a wife and two young daughters alone for an entire winter on Sugar Island in the first quarter of this century!

John returned the following spring with saved wages that allowed him to feed and clothe his family, buy seed, hardware, and quite probably, a cow. John soon found that to do more than simply survive required another source of income. The vast majority of his land was still wooded, with only a few acres cleared. In the 1930's, he began to rent boats, and then boats and motors. Many of his boats were metal. Some he built himself, and the others he easily maintained since he was a tinsmith by trade.

Perhaps the "heyday" of Keko's Place, as it came to be known, was during World War II. Servicemen stationed in the Sault were transported to Keko's boat livery by the truckload, for a relaxing day of fishing. Ask any vet who was stationed in the Sault at the time and chances are he'll tell you about having to wait his turn to rent a boat and motor for 50 cents a day at Keko's Place.

Jussi (John) Keko with a large muskie, ca. 1940s (courtesy of Bill & Nancy Saunders).

Granddaughter Nancy Kauppi was a familiar sight to many fisherman at Keko's Place during the late thirties and early forties, not so shyly asking all:" Hey mister, want to buy some worms?" Many remember today, heading out from Keko's Place for a day of fishing, with a two day supply of worms.

The Kekos continued to run the boat livery until the late 1950s, at which time it was leased to a man from the Sault. John Keko died in 1961; Milja Keko was 101 years old when she died in 1986.

The Niskanen family arrived by way of Chicago. They had immigrated to the United States in 1915. In 1921, Henry Niskanen bought land on the Hay Point road and began farming. He was attracted to this area after reading enthusiastic letters about it in the Finnish language newspaper *Tyomies,* or "Working Man." Marie (Niskanen) Maleport recalled that her mother, sister and she visited the island for four summers beginning in 1921, coming by train from Chicago to the Soo, and then taking the steamer *Elva* to Walker's at Nine Mile Point. They stayed in a tent on the land her father was farming. "One of the first buildings Dad built was a sauna!", she told me. The Orasma, Salo, and Heino families also came to the island from Chicago.

Haying at the Keko farm ca. mid 1920s. Left to right: Gwen Keko, Elsi Holli, John and Milja Keko. The horse was named "Snippy" (courtesy of Bill & Nancy Saunders).

"Sugar Island Band," back row, left to right: Reino Saari, Toivo Koski, Andrew Kuusisto, Sulo Rekola. Front row, Walter Kinney, Bill Tamminen, Larry Hokkanen, Arvo Kuusisto, ca. 1931 (courtesy of Larry & Sylvia Hokkanen).

Farmer's Hall, or the "Finn Hall" as it was popularly known, was built in 1925 and became a social center for this group of islanders. Marie told of going to dances there:"It was accordion music at the Finn Hall, and fiddle music at the town hall. Everybody went to both places and had fun." There were also dance platforms at Whipple Point and one off the Hay Point Road, according to Marie.

There was a Finnish Club in Sault Ste. Marie, Michigan, which disbanded in the late twenties. The instruments from the band which they had had were brought down to Farmer's Hall on Sugar Island. Larry Hokkanen organized the group shown in the accompanying picture. They practiced diligently and put on a performance at the Hall, which was "generously received", but the band broke up shortly thereafter. Larry told of skiing up to Brassar (about 8 miles) several times with his trumpet strapped to his back, to take lessons from Toby Tiihonen, who played in the Sault Symphony Band at the time.

Farmer's Hall was built on one acre of land donated for the purpose by Frank Kuusisto, an island farmer. Actual construction was done by volunteer labor, and much of the lumber used was from trees cut on the island and sawn at a mill on Whipple Point which was run as a cooperative by a group of Finnish men from the island (see illustration of stock certificate). The men who laid the flooring had dancing in mind - over the subfloor they nailed furring strips and then laid the hardwood flooring on top of those strips, which made the finished floor have some "give" to it, thus making an especially nice dancing surface. The hall also served as a gymnasium for the Finnish youth to practice gymnastics and basketball. There were two backboards and as Lawrence Hokkanen told me, "It was pretty close quarters in there for a game."

A recently published book, *Karelia: A Finnish-American Couple in Stalin's Russia, 1934-1941*, was written by Lawrence and Sylvia (Kuusisto) Hokkanen of Sugar Island. Both of their families came to the island about 1920. Speaking of the hall in the book, Sylvia says:

There were dances, sporting events and plays, some comedies, and some with a political message, always leftist.

As the Hokkanens explain in the book, a number of Finnish families on Sugar Island (as elsewhere) were politically active in either the Socialist or Communist Party. This activity was practiced openly, evidently without causing very much reaction among other islanders.

The Hokkanens were recruited along with many other Finnish people in the United States and Canada to go to the Soviet Republic of Karelia to help develop the area. The book describes their seven year stay, which was to become an ordeal full of extreme hardship and fear for their safety. Their story is a fascinating one; although it doesn't deal directly with Sugar Island very often, the book does give the reader a view of a piece of island history that probably few are aware of, unless they have some connection with that era.

Stock Certificate from Sugar Island Co-Operative Association, a group of ten Finnish islanders who operated a sawmill at Whipple Point on Lake George (courtesy Lawrence & Sylvia Hokkanen).

Joe Pete

The mixture of white and Native American people on the island did not occur without friction. In 1929, a book entitled *Joe Pete* was published. The author was Florence McClinchey, a member of the faculty of the English Department at Central Michigan University from 1928 until her death in 1946 as the result of injuries suffered in an automobile accident. McClinchey had spent a number of summers at her cottage on Sugar Island and had established strong ties with some of the Native American islanders. Although the book is a work of fiction, some of the characters are based on people she knew. Sugar Island is not explicitly mentioned in the book, but there is no doubt that it is the island on which the story is set. It depicts the struggle of a Native American woman to raise her son, Joe Pete, in a situation of utter poverty, having been abandoned by the boy's father. The cultural clash between Native American and white is presented - the villain of the tale is a greedy lumberman and land speculator named Jaakola, whom Joe Pete comes to hate because of his relationship with his mother. A Native American man named Big John has high hopes for Joe Pete to become a leader of his people. He looks after the boy and his family and defends Joe Pete in several confrontations with Jaakola. The book is a very moving one, because of the issues it confronts. It was reviewed in such publications as *The New York Times, The Saturday Review of Literature, The Boston Herald*, and others, and was the Christmas Selection of the Book League of America, a leading book club of that era. The American poet Robert Frost was quoted in the publisher's advertisement for the book in *The New York Times* as follows: "It is a new region - a new realm -rarely heard from. Joe Pete is the poor red man with the shadow dark upon him of the white man". A review in *The Boston Transcript* dated Feb. 8, 1930 noted:

> Unusual characters appear. The book deals not romantically but honestly with the Ojibway Indians of Northern Michigan. The author portrays with stark and sympathetic realism the appealing personality of Joe Pete, a full-blooded Indian, as he grows up through an unfortunate boyhood to face the grim tragedy which is the twentieth century life of his people... The book may be propaganda, but if so, it is a sincere presentation of the tragedy of the modern Indian vainly trying to adjust him-

A group of island women at a baby shower held at Pete and Evelyn Maleport home. Back row, left to right: Nellie Adams, Marie Maleport, Pearl Arbic, Ruth Currie, Lucy McIntosh, Hazel Fox, unidentified, Dolly Leask, Mary Solway, Frances Smith, Celina DeLisle, Mamie Thompson, Susan Niskanen, Mary Cairns. Front row: (kneeling), Leona Leask, Sarah Kangas, Elisha McIntosh, (standing), Emma Hytinen, (kneeling), Anna King, Vera Stephenson, Margaret Adams, Harriet McFarlane, Blanche Cox. Children, from left: Earline McIntosh, Dorothy Roy, Barbara Maleport, Beth Maleport, Dale Maleport.

self to a civilization which he can never hope to endure, let alone comprehend.

At the time Miss McClinchey was killed, she was working on a sequel to *Joe Pete*, that was to have been called *Big John*.

From the foregoing, one can see that over the years the population of the island has been an interesting mixture of ethnic backgrounds, the predominant groups having been Native American, French Canadian, Scottish and Finnish.

The preceding discussion has dealt with the people who have made the island their permanent home over the years. It must be noted that during the summer, the population of the island swells considerably, and this influx has occurred for some time. Tax records for Sugar Island Township in 1916 list the following owners of land in the "Bonne Vista Subdivision" near the southeastern tip of the island: John Wesley May, L.C. Sabin, Merlin Wiley, William Miles, Hadie Supe, F.H. Husband, C. Shultz, and A.E. Marriott. Not all of these people had cottages on their land as early as 1916, but evidently the Husbands and Supes did. By about 1920, there were cottages on the Niles, Sabin, Wiley and Marriott properties. Since there were no roads to the area at that time, people got to their property by boat, many of them going in one of Elmo Kibby's launches to the Rain's Dock, which was about a mile away from their cottages.

Foard's Spring Subdivision also existed in 1916, with the same tax records showing property owned by Isabella French, Thomas Foard, Fred Townsend, Robert Cowan, E. Sudendorf, David Povey and George Bailey. This subdivision is on the northwest side of the island, and at least some of these property owners had cottages there.

An early plan to develop a summer resort facility on Sugar Island was described in a booklet published in 1915 by the Chippewa Resort Management, a firm based in Kalamazoo, Michigan, and owned by Ward J. Miller and P. R. Treau. The firm planned to develop a 600 acre resort on the west side of the island, south of Shingle Bay. The property was platted, and according to their booklet, the owners intended to spend $250,000 improving it, complete with a large hotel as the centerpiece. Thus, efforts to develop the island's potential as recreational property began before World War I. As with the cottages, the only access to the resort would have been by boat, of course. Current plat books still show a large tract owned by Chippewa Resort.

In addition to summer visitors from the Sault Ste. Marie area, people came from greater distances as the automobile made such travel more convenient. Reports of the good fishing drew early summer visitors from Ohio to the island. One of them was Carl Secrest, who first visited Sugar Island in the summer of 1933. His family had been fishing in the Alpena area, when they heard of the fabulous fishing to be had near Sugar Island. Their party set out for the island, arriving during the night and with no place to stay. They were told, "Go see Emil Hytinen, he'll put you up." Carl said the Hytinens, who didn't have any kind of resort or rental properties, did indeed put them up in their home, and Secrest's party returned to stay with them for the next four summers as well. He still remembers Mrs. Hytinen's freshly baked biscuits and pumpernickel bread. Carl has only missed spending some time on Sugar Island for one summer since 1933, even managing to visit while in the army during World War II. He and his bride Pauline spent their honeymoon on the island in 1949, bringing with them 22 of the wedding guests!

This chapter has dealt with the people of the island. I hope it has conveyed some of the hard work, courage and vision it took for the pioneers to settle there. I'll leave the last word to Bill and Nancy Saunders:

Today, many of the old farms are overgrown, returned to the woods they once were. Barns have disappeared as have some of the original settlers' homes. The Finn Hall, once the host of dances, parties and political meetings for the Finnish community, stands neglected and in disrepair. But if you go to Keko's old place and walk down by the shore on a summer morning with the sun rising over the Canadian shore, listen carefully. If you do, you may hear this faint echo saying, "Hey mister, want to buy any worms?"

V. Island Institutions

Because the boundary ot the island is so clearly defined by the water surrounding it, Sugar Island is easily thought of as one community. During the early years of its settlement, separate parts of the island probably had more contact with adjacent areas on the mainland than with other parts of the island. Certainly that was the case with the Payment area and its connections with the Garden River area in Ontario. "Mooney" Sebastian related how he often went to a store near Garden River to buy supplies that were cheaper there than in the United States. One time on returning from Canada with some goods, he was met at the shore of the island by two U.S. Customs men. Asked what he was bringing back, Mooney answered "Flour and chicken feed." "Next time, at least cross at night!" he was told.

Post Offices

At least six different post offices operated on the island at one time or another, usually in a store in the respective settlements. The following information about them was taken from the books *Michigan Place Names* by Walter Romig and *Upper Michigan Postal History and Postmarks*, by William J. Taylor.

Baie de Wasai P.O.: First established Aug. 5, 1908 with Alexander Atkins as postmaster. Closed June 30, 1911. Reopened by Ambrose E. Thibert Dec. 11, 1915, and closed Oct. 31, 1943.

Brassar: Opened Mar. 18, 1911 with Urban Nightingale as postmaster. Closed Nov. 30, 1939.

Homestead: Opened May 23, 1906 with Charles Schulz as postmaster. Closed Dec. 31, 1945

Laramie: opened Nov. 18, 1906, with Albert Laramie nominated postmaster. He declined, but Mrs. Delia Laramie accepted the position and operated the post office from the Laramie home. Closed Sept. 15, 1917. The postcard shown in the accompanying photograph was written on a freighter somewhere in Lake Huron by Elmer Pearce, who was sailing on a freighter then, to his young brother Charlie, who was living with his family near the Laramie home. Note the Canal Station postmark, as well as the Laramie postmark. The Canal Station is at the Sault Locks. The Laramie Post Office was located on the St. Marys River where West Shore Drive and Six Mile Road come together.

Payment: opened 12/19/1892 with James S. Shields as first postmaster. Closed Sept. 30, 1942. This was the post office that operated for the longest time.

Willwalk: Opened Feb. 27, 1917 with William Walker as first postmaster. Supposedly Mr. Walker submitted two other names to the post office department first, but they were rejected -— so he joined pieces of his own name and became part of the island's geography. Closed Oct. 16, 1929.

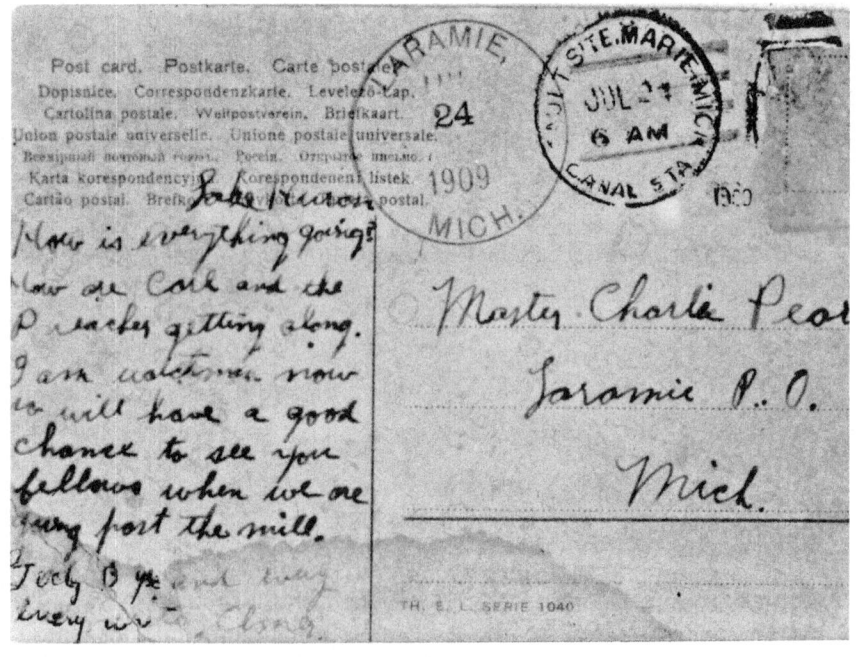

Postcard written by Elmer Pearce on a steamboat in Lake Huron to his brother Charlie. The postmarks are from Canal Station at the Sault Locks, and the Laramie Post Office on Sugar Island (courtesy Charles Pearce).

Taylor's book also mentions a post office, simply named "Sugar Island", which ran from Jan. 13,1857 until Nov. 9, 1861. This was the first post office on Sugar Island; it was undoubtedly located at Payment, and Michael G. Payment was the postmaster.

Mail was brought by boat to each of the post offices three times per week, at least during the twenties and thirties, and island residents picked up their mail at the post office. Marie (Niskanen) Maleport's family moved to Sugar Island in 1921. Their farm was on the Hay Point Road, and they got their mail at Baie de Wasai. "My sister and I walked to the Baie to get the mail in the summer; that was about 5 miles each way, but it was a nice way to pass some time. In the winter, we skied to the post office".

The accompanying photograph was taken from a vantage point that must have been quite close to the post office at Brassar Point. The boat carrying mail probably landed at the dock out on the point.

Abe Laramie told me that his grandmother (Delia, who was postmistress of Laramie post office) spoke French and English when she came to the island and learned to get along in Ojibwa as well; sometimes Native American islanders who couldn't read or write asked her to write letters for them and read the answers when they came back.

Loss of post offices is not at all unique to Sugar Island. According to the *National Geographic Historical Atlas of the United States*, the nation had 76,945 post offices in 1901; the number had declined to 29,557 by 1985, which was about the same number as there were in 1860.

As with post offices, there were schools at each of the different settlements on the island. I have been unable to document dates when the various schools were established; the earliest reference to a school on the island that I have found is contained in a letter dated August 7, 1856, from Indian Agent M.C. Gilbert at Detroit to Mr. Placidus Ord in Sault Ste. Marie:

Sir:

I understand that the Indians residing near Mr. Church -Garden Island [sic] are desirous that a school should be established among them. If you can make an arrangement with them that will be satisfactory, I will appoint you a teacher there -with a salary of $400.00, and am willing to allow $500.00 if the Department at Washington will assent to it.

Very Respectfully,
M.C. Gilbert Indian Agent

I was unable to determine if Mr. Ord actually was hired. The reference to "Garden Island" is apparently the result of Gilbert's confusing the Indian settlement at nearby Garden River with Sugar Island.

At the Chippewa County Register of Deeds Office is a record of a land sale in 1863 by Philetus Church to Sugar Island School District #1, which was at Payment, so evidently there was a public school on Sugar Island at that early date.

Each school district was operated by its own school committee, which consisted of three members -- the Director, the Moderator, and the Assessor or Treasurer. These school committees had a large measure of autonomy, but were all under the supervision of the County School Commissioner. Some very early records of the meetings of the school committee for District No. 1 have been preserved by Mrs. Rose Menard, and made available to me by her son Joe Menard. They cover the period from 1880 through 1916. The committee met once per year. The complete minutes of the 1881 meeting follow:

Brassar Point in the early 1930s (courtesy Sylvia Hovey).

Pursuant to constitutional notice and according to School Act, the annual School Meeting was convened in the place where the school is kept, on the first Monday of September, 1881, at 7 P.M.

On motion John Sebastian Senior was elected Moderator to fill out E.J. Pink's unexpired term, whose office was ruled vacant.

On motion P.S. Church, Esq. was re-elected Director of the District for the ensuing three years.

On motion it became the law of the District that for the ensuing year we have school for eight months; and by vote it was decided that we hire a female teacher.

The census (of school age children in the district) taken by Miss Victoria Payment was submitted and approved. A verbal report was made that an ineffectual effort was made to organize other school districts on the Island and advice asked as to the proper course to pursue to effect the division. The applicants were referred to the School Manual.

The Director presented his accounts as follows. The meeting ruled the statements as correct. Result: Balance due P.S. Church $35.22

It was voted that the one mill tax be the law for the ensuing year.

On motion the Director was instructed to purchase books for the poor children in the District attending the school who were not supplied sufficiently and were unable to buy them, and the money for such purpose be taken from the one mill tax.

The Moderator and Director signed the required declaration of acceptance of office and the meeting adjourned.

Officers:
P.S. Church   Director 3 years
John Sebastian   Moderator 2 years
David Tate   Assessor 1 year

Sugar Island
September 5, 1881

The meeting recorded above was longer than most meetings of that era. Each year a decision had to be made about how long school would be in session, and how much tax would be levied. The two decisions were intimately related, and the length of the school year varied from four months (1889-90) to ten months (1911-12) in the period from 1880 to 1916. The teacher was paid $25 per month in the 1880s, and the salary had risen to $35 per month by 1910. The uncertainties of the situation are illustrated by the following excerpt from the minutes of the meeting in 1898:

Moved by John Sebastian and seconded by Angus McCoy that we have two months school this fall and three in the spring, provided that we find a teacher willing to wait until spring for pay.

Over the years, the school committees of District No. 1 were not afraid to try different ways of doing things. The five month year noted above, split between fall and spring, probably had a four month recess from November through February. That would lessen the amount of firewood needed to heat the building; also, some children probably had to travel long distances to get to school, and the winter months would make such travel more difficult - indeed, more hazardous.

The school year of 1889-90 was an unusual one. That year, no school was held at all during the fall and winter. A special meeting of the school committee was held in April and it was decided to have four months of school, starting May 1, with a one month recess from July 15 to August 15. The school year would then have finished by the end of September — just in time for the start of the 1890-91 school year, as it turned out!

Records at the Register of Deeds office indicate that in 1887, Annie Crushier sold a parcel of land to School District #2, at Brassar. The "ineffectual efforts" to organize another school district on the Island were noted in the minutes of the 1881 meeting above, so evidently sometime between 1881 and 1887 those efforts paid off, with the formation of District #2.

A letter dated March 25, 1889, written by the Chippewa County Board of School Examiners to the School Board of District #4 (Baie de Wasai) was shown to me by Mary Murray. The letter concerned the granting of a special certification of a teacher named Mrs. W. Kinney to teach at the Baie school.

Thus, there were at least four school districts on the island as early as 1889.

By 1902, there were five school districts on the island; the numbering of the districts evidently corresponds to the sequence in which they were established:

District #1	Payment
District #2	Brassar
District #3	Roosevelt (later called Edison School serving the area roughly from the center to the east side of the island, from one and one-half mile road south to about four mile road)
District #4 :	Baie de Wasai (Harding School)
District #5 :	Willwalk (Hiawatha School)

Minutes of the school committee meetings for District #3 from 1922 through 1937 have also survived. In these more recent times, the annual meetings were still quite short. In fact, they had changed little from those of fifty years earlier, such as the proceedings of the 1881 meeting recorded above. The main decisions were still the length of the school year, how much tax to levy, how much to pay the teacher, and whose bid to accept for firewood to heat the school ($6.25 per double cord of hardwood was the going rate). The effects of the depression years can be seen in the salaries paid the teacher at the Edison School. In 1929 Edison's teacher was paid $100 per month.

From 1933 through 1937, my father, Pete Arbic, taught there; he was paid $75 per month and, of course, was considered lucky to have a job.

Other than the salary that was to be paid, there is almost no mention of the teachers in the available minutes. Based on my interviews with older islanders, it appears that typically a young woman would be hired, and she often boarded with a family near the school. More than once, the arrangement ultimately led to a marriage between the teacher and one of the boys in the family.

Records at the Eastern Upper Peninsula Intermediate School District office in Sault Ste. Marie document all of the teachers in the rural schools of Chippewa County from 1902 into the nineteen forties. The list below indicates who taught at each of the five Sugar Island schools in 1902 and for how many months school was held:

District 1   Mary McKechnie; 5 months
District 2   Mary Abel; 5 months
District 3   Mae Bunker; 7 months
District 4   Lavina Kelcher; 6 months
District 5   Margaret Kelley; 6 months

The tremendous turnover of teachers in island schools is apparent when these records are examined over a period of years. For example, over the eight school years 1902-1903 through 1909-1910 there were a total of 43 different teachers who taught at one of the five schools on Sugar Island! That means that essentially, there was a new teacher at each school each of those years and three left over (several teachers didn't stay for a full year). Only one teacher taught for three consecutive years in island schools during that eight year period. This extreme turnover, by the way, appears to have been typical throughout the county schools then. I have been told that there were social pressures against a married woman teaching, creating a two-income family when jobs were scarce. If that was the case, such pressures would have increased the turnover. By the 1930s, the turnover rate had lessened somewhat, but was still very high.

Both of my parents taught at island schools - my mother, Pearl (Schopp) Arbic, at Baie de Wasai in 1930-31 and 1934-35; my father at the Edison School from 1933-36 and Baie de Wasai in 1936-37. Mother boarded with Gene Thibert's family at the Baie store before her marriage. Dad boarded with the Alfred DeLisle family part of the time and told me that after Mr. DeLisle watched him eat a few times he exclaimed, "I'd rather pay your board than feed you!" While he was courting my mother, Dad liked to bring his students down to her school for a spelling bee. I expect that year the island produced some pretty good spellers.

The district school board would pay the teacher an extra amount, perhaps $8.00 per month, if he or she would serve as janitor, getting to school early enough to light the stove and warm up the building. Sometimes, one of the older students took that job. Virginia (Solway) Roy remembered one day at the Edison School when the older boys didn't want to attend classes. They climbed into the attic and stuffed the chimney full of rags before they built the fire, hoping to smoke out school that day. The teacher arrived just in time to foil the plans of the reluctant scholars. In a similar vein, Bill Marks told me that one year when he was going to school at Willwalk a fellow student had been contracted to provide transportation to the students who lived quite a distance south of the school. It seems that a few times during the winter when school didn't seem like the best way to spend the day, the youthful transportation officer and his fellow students "accidentally" wound up in a snowbank and naturally there was no point continuing on to school by the time they managed to get the car out.

Virginia Roy started school at age five. As she had no close neighbor children, she walked to school by herself:

> I walked two miles there, and two miles back. If there was a storm, one of the parents would come and meet us — but it had to be real bad before they bothered with us — we were tough! Then the Korpis moved in nearby, so I had Ella and Elsie to walk with. We had a big old box stove that took three-foot wood; when it was real cold, we sat around the stove with our backs to it, and then had to turn around and warm up our front sides. Our sandwiches would get frozen, so the teacher had the idea that each of us would bring some vegetables or a piece of meat from home, and we threw it all together in a pot and cooked a stew for lunch. We had our own home-made hot lunch program.

Schools provided an opportunity for social life among the adults of the communities as well. Virginia recalled that "box socials" were common when she was growing up on the island.

All the women made a nice lunch and brought it to a dance in a nicely decorated box. Usually, the bachelors would manage to find out which one the teacher had brought, and they would bid it up really high when the lunches were auctioned off— sometimes going as high as eight dollars — so they could eat lunch with the teacher, and dance the first dance afterward with her! The money raised was often used to help pay school operating costs.

My mother recalled that during the Christmas season each school put

KINNEY'S SHOE STORE
Wishes You a Joyful Christmas
SHOES FOR THE ENTIRE FAMILY

SOO THEATRE -- SUN. - TUE.
DEC. 24 - 26
"SITTING PRETTY"
With Jack Oakie - Jack Haley - Ginger Rogers and Pickens Sisters

Program

1. The Big Welcome .... Clarence Smith
2. The Night Before Xmas .... Dorothy McIntosh
3. Christmas Recipe .... Dorothy Cox
4. Grandma's Gift .... Marie Cox, Douglas Turrell
5. Small Things .... Virginia Williams, Elizabeth Malsport

BEST WISHES
E. Pingatore & Son
SOO'S BUSIEST CLEANERS

IF IT'S A GOOD PICTURE, YOU'LL SEE IT AT THE
COLONIAL THEATRE
WHERE THE TALKIES TALK BEST
3 SHOWS DAILY
2:30   7:15   9:00
MATS. 10c - 20c
EVES. 10c - 25c

BEST WISHES
BAKER'S SHOE SHOP
EXCELLENT REPAIRING

QUALITY BUILDING MATERIALS
L. M. Hollingsworth

Program
Play - "Henry's Mail-Order Wife"
CAST

Billy Murray .... Bud Roy
George Murray .... Fred Currie
Jim Jones .... Donald Thompson
Becky Simpson .... Grace Thompson
Mrs. Tucker .... Ruth Salo
The Minister .... Frank Smith

THE SEASON'S GREETINGS
Remember Us When in Need of Hardware
The Soo Hardware Co.

THE HUB
Store of Quality
REASONABLE PRICES

COMPLIMENTS
Soo Builders Supply Co.

MERRY CHRISTMAS
J. L. Lipsett & Son

Program
Play - "The Cycle of the Year"
CAST

New Year .... Leo Laakso
January .... Dorothy McIntosh
February .... Marie Cox
March .... George Currie
April .... Dorothy Cox
May .... Ethel Smith
June .... Ruth Salo
July .... Stanley Smith
August .... Douglas Turrell
September .... Clarence Smith
October .... Virginia Williams
November .... Arnold Williams
December .... Edwin Saarni

SOO'S LEADING SHOE STORE
Wishes you a Merry Xmas
PASSMORE'S

SEASON'S GREETINGS
Gowan Hardware Co.

Edison School Christmas Program, 1933 (courtesy Carol (Arbic) Flinn).

106

on a Christmas program —" on a different night, of course. That way, people from different parts of the island could attend several of the programs." (No television in those days). No doubt, a certain amount of friendly competition prevailed among the teachers to put on a good program.

Roosevelt School, ca. 1910. The name of the teacher is not known. Among the students are Pete and Armour Maleport, Blanche (Maleport) Cox, Pearl McKenzie, Leo DeLisle, and Leonard Murray (courtesy Impi Curlis).

A copy of the front of the program from Edison School in 1933 when my father taught there is included. A lot of work went into securing advertisements and printing a fancy program. The play presented that year had the catchy title: "*Henry's Mail-order Wife*" (There is a "mail-order" house on the island. The Murray home, located on Three Mile Road east of the Homestead Road, came from Sears Roebuck and was erected in about 1912. I asked Virginia Roy when the home was erected, because I knew her father, Phil Solway, had helped to build it. She said, "The house and I are almost the same age, because I was just a baby when it was built - I hope I'm holding up better than the house is!")

The oldest school building of which I have a picture is the log school building that sat on "Boulley's Hill, up from Laramie's place." The picture was taken in 1908 and was obtained from Charlie Pearce, who attended the school a few years after that. This school was attended by children from the area between Six Mile and Nine Mile roads. Angus Gurnoe was among them and he lived more than three miles away. Angus confessed that sometimes on a good sliding day in the winter he and some friends never quite made it to school. Some time just prior to 1920 a new school to serve the children of this area was built at Willwalk. After that time, the log schoolhouse served as a home for Hector MacGilivry for several years. It burned sometime after 1924, according to information contained in an article about the school written by Deidre Stevens and published in the August 23, 1984 issue of *The Evening News*:

> The Laramie school was a log building, plastered and white-washed on the outside, with two windows on either side that were perpetually broken, and a ceiling covered with white building paper, according to Charlie Pearce, one of its only surviving students. It was heated by an iron woodstove in one corner....
>
> Some of the students came to school by dogsled in the winter, parking the sleds outside. During classes the dogs wandered through the broken windows, sleeping by the stove until another sled should go by on its way to the mainland past the school. Then up the dogs would go, and out the windows, running after the sleds. When the sleds had gone by,

they would return. And through all this excitement, the teacher was attempting to proceed as usual.

Abe Laramie also attended the school that bore his name. He remembers the ceiling a bit differently than Charlie, indicating that it was RED building paper rather than white. But it was definitely paper nailed to a framework, with no structural material between the rafters. Abe told me, "One day, Norman Boulley and Freddie Oller, two of the older students, crawled up there during recess and went to sleep perched on the rafters. One of them rolled over in his sleep and came crashing down through the paper ceiling after classes had resumed."

Abe told me that the Boulley family had a billygoat named "Ten

Log Schoolhouse on "Boulley's Hill" (Six Mile Rd.) ca. 1909. The teacher was Mary (Barkley) Pearce. Among the students were Fred Pearce, Louise (Boulley) Smith, Ethel (Pearce) Curtis, and Stella (Boulley) Harper (courtesy Charles Pearce).

Cents". The goat, which had a fragrance all its own, liked to follow children into the school after they had made a trip to the outdoor toilet. "The kids were all for this kind of excitement."

Abe told me," and the teacher sometimes had quite a job to get the goat outside, because he was one of those 'bumpers', you know."

Some of the students and teachers on the island skied to school in the winter, as shown in the next photograph. My father claimed that he could "roll a cigarette one-handed in a northwest wind" while crossing fields to get to Edison School. Lauri Karimo, a Finnish immigrant on the island, made many pairs of skis and sold them for $15.00 a pair.

Since eighth grade was the highest grade ever taught on the island, any student wishing to continue beyond that level had to attend school on the mainland. Prior to 1937, such students usually went to school in Sault Ste. Marie, taking room and board with a family there. In 1937, the school districts on the island consolidated into a single unit and this move enabled the larger school district to provide transportation for island students to go to high school in Sault Ste. Marie. The school board for Sugar Island in 1937 consisted of Len Fox, John Orasma, Bert McKerchie, William Sebastian and John Williams.

Roosevelt School, ca. 1925, showing how the teacher and some students got there. Their identities are unknown to the author. Photograph by Sylvia Hovey.

As island population declined, the schools at Willwalk, Payment and Baie de Wasai closed. Beginning in 1952, grades K-3 were consolidated to the Edison school, with grades 4-8 being taught at Brassar. In 1959, the Brassar school closed and the Willwalk school was moved to the site of the Edison school, so that two buildings were on the same site. Grades K-8 were taught there with June Boyer sharing the job with several other teachers during the following six years. In 1965, island residents voted to join the Sault school district, hoping in the process that a new school building would be constructed on the island. Grades K-3 were still taught on the island while students from grade 4 up were bussed to the Sault. In the fall of 1966, the furnace at the school broke down, and for five weeks the seventeen K-3 youngsters were transported to the Sault's Finlayson school while the furnace was replaced. In 1966, Project: WILDS (Worthwhile Ideas for Learning Development on Sugar Island) was presented to the Sault Ste. Marie School Board by Benjamin Jones and Robert Beecroft. This plan called for the construction of a two-room school building and at the same time the design of a curriculum tied to the history and unique natural history of the island. The proposal was never implemented and in June, 1969, the final classes were held on the island, with June Boyer as the teacher. Since then all children have been transported to the mainland for school.

Churches

An entry from Bishop Frederic Baraga's diary, contained in *History of the Diocese of Sault Ste. Marie and Marquette* reads:

August 28, 1854 Went to Paiment (sic) and confirmed there 44 Indians and others.

A later reference to Sugar Island in the book states

.... in Perault's landing he made arrangements for a new church.

This refers to the Holy Angels Church at Payment, which was built in 1856-57 by Michael G. Payment, according to an article dated August 12, 1982, in *The Evening News*. The church had been placed on the National Register of Historic Places just prior to the publishing of the article. The entry in the diary for February 3, 1857 is:

> Spent the day in Payment; in the evening, prayed and preached in French, at Payment.

There are numerous references to Sugar Island in Baraga's diary, especially after he began efforts to construct a new mission church at the Indian settlement on the shore of Lake George opposite Gem Island. Baraga referred to this settlement as "Minisheing"; Wayne State University press recently published *Diary of Bishop Frederic Baraga*, edited and with annotations by Regis Walling and Rev. N. Daniel Rupp. A footnote in that volume contains the following agreement between Baraga and the Indians who lived at Minisheing:

> Bishop Frederic Baraga and Shawabinessi, and all the Indians who live here at Point of Peninsula, all of them are happy that a Catholic church was built here in their village, and that one acre of land was selected to have here a church. Of this land and the church, no one will be the only owner, all together will own it; the priest will own it, so that he may say Mass here, and that he may preach here, and do all that the priest thinks he must do; but the Indians will own it, to worship there, and that they do all the things as much as they think Catholic Christians must do. The priest will never be able to sell it; and the Indians who are living here now, and who will be praying here (those who will be Christians) will not be able to sell this piece of land and the church.

I spoke with Regis Walling, co-editor of the *Baraga Diary*, about this quotation, indicating to her my admiration for the language in it, which I consider to be elegant in its clarity and simplicity. She told me that it is the only agreement of this nature, between a priest and a congregation, that she has ever come across.

Later in the *Diary*, another footnote contains excerpts of a letter Baraga wrote to the Leopoldine Society in Vienna:

To my great consolation and spiritual joy I have also founded a new mission and built a mission church on the so-called Sugar Island, on [the] Saint Mary's River, 20 English miles away from Sault Ste. Marie. Here is a small settlement of Indians, some of whom are already baptized. Others are still pagans. In order to provide them with a better opportunity to become converted, and to attain their eternal salvation, I had a small church built, which, on Oct. 27 [1861] I blessed to God under the name St. Joseph. The church was full of Christians and pagans and all were pleased that in this desolate and remote Indian location, a church now

St. Joseph's Mission Church near Gem Island, ca. 1930 (courtesy of Bayliss Public Library).

stands in which the sublime sacrifice of the New Testament is offered and the holy sacraments are administered, and where they hear the redeeming truths of the Christian religion in their own native language.

The church was built by two island men, Edward Perrault and his son Joseph, largely of wood sawn on the island at Philetus Church's sawmill. Incidentally, Joseph and Edward were respectively maternal great-grandfather and grandfather of Mary Murray (see chapter 4). Baraga himself built the tabernacle, baptismal font and a stand for books.

West of the church, atop a steep-sided knoll, can still be found the "Gem Island Cemetery." When I visited the cemetery in the summer of 1991, it was very overgrown. A few gravestones could be found, and several other graves were marked with wooden crosses. A passage in the book *Joe Pete* describes a funeral procession to this cemetery. Ed Pine indicated that his grandfather, Ed Boulley, was buried in the Gem Island Cemetery in 1948 and was the last to be buried there. The church itself still stood until about 1940, but it had not been used for some years prior to that date.

Father William Gagnieur was another priest well-known and beloved by older islanders. Leslie Atkins told me that Father Gagnieur would stop at Baie de Wasai (this would be about 1910) when he was "making his rounds", often staying the night with the LaCoy family. The next day he would celebrate mass at the Baie school, which would be dismissed for the morning if it happened to be a school day. He also visited the lumber camps to say mass. Like others of the time, he got to the island by small boat or crossed the ice if it was winter, often carrying his altar equipment on his back. Adelaide Thibert told me that "Father Gagnieur drowned many times!" She was referring to the many times he went through the ice while crossing to or from the island.

An article about Father Gagnieur was published December 22, 1929 in *The Detroit Free Press* under the title "The Last Missionary." The article relates that Father Gagnieur came to Manitoulin Island from Montreal in about 1890; the following is from the article:

Father Gagnieur lived on Manitoulin Island for four years. Most of the time was spent wandering up and down the north shore of the St. Mary's and among the scattered islands about Manitoulin by snowshoe and dogsled in winter and by canoe in summer. Traveling in this region in the winter and springtime in those days was no easy matter. The woods in winter were covered with from four to five feet of snow, and knee-deep slush confronted the wayfarer in the spring break-up. Blizzards often added to the hardship. Caught in one of these one winter night in 1891, the missionary, half dead and with his feet frozen, was dragged to safety by his dogs.

... He came to the Sault in 1895 and has remained here. He is still in charge of the Indian missions. What will become of these missions when the Jesuit is gone is a matter of conjecture. Whoever takes charge of

Father Gagnieur outside Sacred Heart Church at Baie de Wasai, after the baptism of infant Betty Lou Phillips, held by her godfather Fred Hatch, with godmother Polly Cadotte, ca. 1932 (courtesy Mary Murray).

them must know the Indian languages, and they are very difficult to master... Father Gagnieur says he is still attempting to master the more than 200,000 words of the Chippewa language.... He speaks French as well as English and Indian, and is a talented musician.

Father Gagnieur served missions in the Upper Peninsula as far west as Nahma until his death in 1937. His successor was Father Paul Prud'homme. Father Joseph Lawless came to the eastern Upper Peninsula area in 1946 at the request of Father Prud'homme, who required help to serve the needs of Native Americans throughout most of the Upper Peninsula. Fr. Lawless told me that Fr. Prud'homme " knew every Indian in the Upper Peninsula." In the tradition of Bishop Baraga, who has been called the "Snowshoe Priest", and Fr. Gagnieur, Fr. Prud'homme came to the Sault from his mission at Goulais Bay in Ontario on snowshoes to attend the funeral of Fr. Gagnieur in 1937. He would have covered between 15 and 20 miles to get to the funeral.

Sacred Heart Church at Baie de Wasai was built in 1925 under the direction of Fr. William Gagnieur.

Another mission church on the island was the Church of Ste. Theresa. The building was about 12 by 16 feet and was located on the west shore of the island, near Six Mile Road. About 1940, it was moved to the Willwalk area where it was used for a short while. In 1949, a larger structure named St. John and Ste. Anne Church was built in its place. In a subsequent consolidation effort about 1960, this building was moved to Baie de Wasai to become an addition to the Sacred Heart Church structure.

It appears that Fr. Joseph Lawless, with 45 years of service in the area at the time this book is being written, will be the last in the long line of Jesuit priests offering pastoral services in the Sault Ste. Marie area. The Jesuit Order, Detroit District, has informed the Diocese of Marquette that it can no longer support a mission in the area. As of June, 1992, Sacred Heart Church will fall under the auspices of St. Mary's Pro-Cathedral in Sault Ste. Marie.

There were Protestant missionary efforts on Sugar Island as well. The Michigan Home Mission Society owned land at Payment in the 1880's. A visit to Sugar Island by Rev. W.G. Puddefoot, Field Secretary of the Congregational Home Mission Society, is described in Puddefoot's book *The Minute Man on the Frontier*. A chapter entitled "A Sunday on Sugar Island" offers a fascinating glimpse into the island's past:

> It was eight miles to our first appointment, and we went by water. Mrs. Scurr and the two children, with a little maid, made up our company, so that our boat was well filled. My hands, not used to rowing, soon gave out, and Brother Scurr had to do nearly all of that work. It was a hot, bright morning in the latter part of June — a lovely day -— and we soon passed down the river into Lake George, and after two hours' steady pulling, we made a landing opposite a log house just vacated by the settlers for one more convenient.
>
> This was our sanctuary for the morning. Here we found a mixed company — settlers from Canada, "the States", Chippewas, etc., men, women, and children. Some of them came four, five and eight miles; some in boats, some on foot. One old Indian was there who did not know a word of English, but sat listening as intently as if he took it all in.

After the sermon and communion service, the group went to another location further south on the Lake George shoreline:

> Another good pull at the oar and a little help from the wind brought us to our second stage, the Indian village. On the hillside stood the schoolhouse where we were to preach ... We had a somewhat different audience this time, only four white men being present; but all could understand English, except our old Indian friend of the morning, who was again present, and for whose benefit the chief's son arose after I was through, and interpreted the whole discourse, save a little part which he condensed as the time was short. I was both astonished and delighted. The people told me he could do so with a sermon an hour long, without a break. Most of the company, as a rule, understand both languages, and keep up a keen watch for mistakes. It was a wonderful feat. The man's gestures were perfect; he was a natural orator.

The newest church on Sugar Island is St. Luke's On The Trail. This church is located in Homestead on land donated by Dr. and Mrs. Joe Shaeffer that was once part of Allen Rains' farm. The church was designed by the Schaeffer's daughter and son-in-law, Sarah and Floyd Brezavar, both of whom are architects. The dedication service was held August 17, 1986. The structure was built largely of wood cut on the Schaeffer property and sawn by Glen Murray, and most of the labor was done by volunteers. The chairs in the church were donated in memory of various people. There have been requests to provide more, but the church is already full! Eileen Hughes obtained a set of hymnals from her Baptist church in Miamisburg, Ohio, and Jack and Lou Seibert secured a set from their Lutheran church in Wyandotte, Michigan. Stained glass windows in the interior doors at the back of the church were given by Helen Burgess Kraai in memory of her husband, Irv Burgess. They contain references to Sugar Island, beloved by both Helen and Irv. The church stands as a genuine monument to a community spirit and acts as a focus to strengthen the community. The congregation is ecumenical, and folks from the north end of the island attend services there as well as those from the Homestead area.

St. Luke's On The Trail, 1991 (photo by author).

Stores

As with post offices, several stores once supplied islanders' needs when it wasn't so easy to get around.

It is likely that Philetus Church had the first establishment that sold goods to island residents, at Church's Landing. Exact dates aren't available, but the store probably operated from about 1850 to the early 1880s.

Angus McCoy also had a store in the Payment area, which he ran for upwards of 50 years. He started the business before the turn of the century; as with other stores of the era on the island, it also served as a post office. The mail boat from the Sault arrived in the evening and went back uptown the following morning. Angus operated the store it until his death in about 1947. Shortly thereafter, the store was closed, but the building is still standing.

John "Hobo" McFarlane opened a tavern in a log building in Brassar, on the northeast corner of Brassar Road and the road to Brassar Point, in the early 1930s. The building was expanded and converted into a store in 1936 by Donald and Harriet McFarlane. Prominent were hand-operated gas pumps - you could see what you were buying in those days, and it didn't come from OPEC. The store was sold to Joe Leask in 1945, who operated it until about 1950, when it was sold to Leonard and Hazel Fox. The Foxes ran the store until about 1957, at which time Ed and Alice Handziak purchased it, operating it until about 1961. The last owner to run the store was Don Currie, who closed the store a few years later, The building was used as a home for a short time and was destroyed by fire.

Baie de Wasai has had a small store in operation continuously since about 1900. The first store to offer much was run by Alex Atkins, who purchased a smaller operation from a man named McKenzie in 1908. The store was sold to Ambrose "Gene" Thibert about 1914. Gene and his wife Bertha owned the store until 1937. As noted previously, Gene also carried passengers to town and back in his launch three times a week.

The room on the right of the store building contained a pool table which was sometimes moved aside so that Emil Hytinen could practice wrestling with some brave partner. (Emil, a man of legendary strength, was deputy sheriff for a time.)

Thibert sold the store to Hobart ("Hobie") and Jane Norris in 1937. Advertisements in *Brown and Gold*, the Baie de Wasai school newspaper, refer

McFarlane Store at Brassar, ca. 1935, [courtesy Emery & Donna (McFarlane) Corbiere].

Baie de Wasai store and post office, 1933, (courtesy Jo Osmar).

Portion of tourist brochure from the 1930s, at Baie de Wasai. Gene Thibert is on the left of a fine stringer of fish. Fishermen are Lee Farmer (center), and "Mac" MacGregor (right), (courtesy Sylvia Hovey).

Front of tourist brochure from 1930s. Neither of the subjects has been identified, (courtesy Sylvia Hovey).

to the store as "The Trading Post." This name may have been given it by the Norrises when they acquired it. They soon added a tavern next to the store. An advertisement in the Nov. 12, 1937, issue of *Brown and Gold* read:

> Announcing the opening of the new tavern Saturday, Nov. 13!
> Name the tavern and win $2.00. The person submitting the best name for the new tavern will win $2.00 CASH.
> Leave your slip at the Trading Post.
> Contest ends Nov. 20.

The prize winning name was "The Old Stockade," or at least that was the name ultimately given to the tavern and dance hall that was such a lively spot it is still talked about by the older islanders. A tragedy is linked to the Stockade; a car carrying band members who had played at a dance there, sometime in the early 1940s, went off the end of the ferry dock into the river, and two of the members drowned.

The Norrises sold the store to Marie Thibert in 1946, who operated it until 1949, when it was sold to Earlin and Gert Wilds. The Wilds replaced the wooden structure with the present block building and were able to expand the range of goods offered soon thereafter because of the extra space and elec-

The Stockade at Baie de Wasai, in the late 1930s or early 1940s (courtesy of Carl & Pauline Secrest).

trical service, which became available in 1954. I spent the summer of 1955 working for Gert and Earlin at the store. As in many stores of the era, charge accounts were kept for regular customers, but beer and wine couldn't be charged. One afternoon towards the end of the month an old fellow came into the store about two o'clock and charged a paint brush. He came back about four o'clock with the brush and said he'd changed his mind about painting, after all. He asked me for a refund, in cash. Being somewhat wet behind the ears, I was about to comply, but Gert had overheard the request and put a quick stop to any cash refund.

The store is now owned by Ed Belleau, a nephew of Gert and Earlin. He has been running it since 1971.

William Walker ran a store and post office at Willwalk from 1917 until 1929. The building sat out on the end of a long dock near Nine Mile Point. Mail and passengers arrived there regularly. As mentioned in Chapter Four, many newcomers to Sugar Island in the 1920s first set foot on it at Walker's. There was also a dance hall there during the 1930s. I haven't been able to locate a picture of the buildings, but the accompanying photograph shows a por-

Andrew Kuusisto on William Walker's dock at Nine Mile Point ca.1928.

tion of the dock. The store was reported to be quite a bit smaller than the Baie store of the same era.

Gert Kauppi built and operated the store known as "Gertie K's" between the ferry road and Baie de Wasai in the mid to late 1950's. The business was sold in 1972 to Lloyd and Evelyn Drury, who operated it as Lloyd Drury's Service until 1988. At that time it was purchased by William and Linda King. Robert Wilcox purchased the business, then known as King's Service, in 1990 and is the current owner.

The Hilltop Bar must be included among island "institutions." It was built in 1948 by John Adams and Ken Fox. They used one of the hutment buildings left over from the army unit that had been stationed there to house the gasoline powered generator which supplied power to the building. The business was soon sold to Fred and Edith Heller, who ran it for about two years. In 1951, it was purchased by Merlin and Irene McCoy, who ran the bar until 1971. Merlin had a quick wit, as illustrated by the following anecdote. My father sold Ashley woodstoves, one of the early air-tight models, as a sideline. One day in the Hilltop, he was giving his sales pitch to Don Thompson. Dad

The Hilltop Bar, ca. 1955. Standing third from the right is Merlin McCoy, on his right is Earlin Wilds and on his left is Charlie Gardner. The other men are unidentified (courtesy Irene McCoy).

said, "Just think, Don - if you buy one of these stoves, next year you'll only have to cut half as much firewood as this year." Merlin overheard from behind the bar and pitched in with, "You ought to buy two of 'em, Don, then you won't have to cut any wood at all next year!". The Hilltop has been a center of activity on the island for over 40 years now. The owner in 1991 is "The Five D's, Inc." with Steve Miller as the manager.

The Community Center

Since it opened in December, 1977, the Sugar Island Township Community Center has been another focus of community activity. The first senior citizen dinner was held there on December 9, 1977, with about 75 in attendance. Since that time, it has become the meeting place for organizations such as the Sugar Island Lions and Lionesses, the volunteer Ambulance Corps and Fire Department, as well as the Township Board.

The Osborn Preserve

Chase S. Osborn was one of the most prominent men to have been associated with Sugar Island. The Governor of Michigan for one term, 1911-1912, he was also a newspaper publisher, prospector, world traveler, prolific writer, and philanthropist. Born in Indiana, he came to Sault Ste. Marie from Florence, Wisconsin, in 1887. He started a newspaper, *The Sault News*, soon afterward. He was postmaster of Sault Ste. Marie from 1889 to 1893, State Fish and Game Warden from 1895 to 1899, Commissioner of Railroads from 1899-1903, and a member of the Board of Regents of the University of Michigan from 1908 to 1911. He was an early advocate of the idea of bridging the Straits of Mackinac. In 1940, the City of Sault Ste. Marie put on a celebration to honor Osborn, the occasion being his 80th birthday. In connection with that celebration, the city published a 600 page volume entitled *An Accolade for Chase S. Osborn*. The bibliography in that book, listing material written by and about Osborn, is 13 pages long! Although he traveled throughout the world, Sugar Island was one of his favorite places, and he spent virtually every summer at his Duck Island complex from the late 1920s until his death in 1949.

Chase Osborn assembled the parcel of land that was later to become the Osborn Preserve through purchases made over a period of about 15 years beginning in 1908, when he purchased Duck Island and property adjacent to Duck Lake on its west side from Charles Schultz and Charles P. Randall. Others who had owned portions of this shore property earlier were Freeman Dickerson, Harry Marks, Frank Weston, George Kemp, John Hulbert, William Gates and P.M. Church. Major pieces of property with no frontage were purchased from John Joseph, John Greensky and William Gates. Ultimately, his contiguous holdings grew to about 3,000 acres.

In 1929, Chase Osborn and his son George donated this property to the University of Michigan. The terms of the Osborn gift reserved for Chase Osborn during his lifetime the right to the use of Duck Island and its buildings and library. The library, or "Go-Down" as he called it, reminded me of a small jail. It is built of concrete and has only small windows with bars on them to protect the more than 7,000 volumes that it once contained. Some of the books have subsequently been placed in collections at the University of Michigan and at Lake Superior State University. When the gift was presented, Chase Osborn said:

> It is my belief that this gift will be one that will be of everlasting benefit to the University of Michigan. Gifts of money and of buildings and of books will perish in time. These lands, than which there are none more interesting in all of God's world, will be here, amid their setting of grandeur, for all time.

This quotation is from an article by Marshall Shulman, published in the April 5th, 1936, issue of *The Michigan Daily*. That article was written seven years after the University had been given the property, and at the time of its writing, Shulman stated that fewer than a dozen University faculty members had even seen the property by that time. It is a beautiful piece of the island that is nice to have in a sort of public ownership, but it is also 3,000 acres of land including upwards of eight miles of water frontage on which no taxes are paid.

Charley Andrews, one of the last full-blooded Chippewas from the island, worked for Chase Osborn for about 16 years, acting as general handyman, as well as his chauffeur. When Osborn went to "Possum Poke," his

Georgia retreat, Charley accompanied him. Many articles written about Gov. Osborn refer to his right hand man, "Gib," short for "Ne-on-gib", which means "he who rests." (I once asked one of Joe's sons if his uncle Charley had ever married. He told me, "No; he had quite a few cooks, but he never got married"). Charley later worked as general handyman for Gil Nelson at his resort at Homestead. He died in 1985. The image on the cover of the book is a drawing of Charley by my son, Joel Arbic, based on the photograph from the previous page. Joel told me "The wrinkles in his face and neck seemed to blend and become topographical features on the island."

Charley's brother, Joe, became the caretaker of the property shortly after it was given to the University, and acted in that capacity until his retirement in 1976. Joe and his wife Josephine raised 12 children on the island. Not a man of many words (although quick with a smile and soft chuckle), Joe was a challenge to interview, which is what I did in preparing for this book. He did

Charley Andrews in 1982 (photo by Bill Hamilton).

his best to answer my questions, but I didn't have the ability to get him to volunteer stories from his long life on the island. That's my loss as well as that of the reader who didn't know him, for he lived through an interesting time of many changes on the island. I didn't know him well, but remember him from when I worked at the Baie store some 30 years ago, pulling up in a blue University pickup with several children in the back, then coming into the store with them all in tow - calmly making his selections, maintaining order among the children in such a quiet way. He was a true gentleman, and that's the word chosen by so many who knew him, when asked to describe him. Polly Cadotte, about whom Stellanova Osborn wrote a short book in verse of the same name, was the step-mother of Joe and Charley. After Joe's retirement, the caretaking duties fell largely on his daughter Pauline. As of the writing of this book, caretaker duties at the Osborn Preserve have been assigned to Joe's son, Edward Andrews.

VI. More Recently...

United Nations on Sugar Island

Chase S. Osborn was mentioned earlier in connection with the Osborn Preserve. After World War II, when the United Nations was being created, Governor Osborn played a major role in the attempt to have Sugar Island selected as the site for the headquarters of the organization. His argument for such a choice was based primarily on the fact that the island sits on the longest unfortified boundary in the world. Having been the object of a protracted dispute over its ownership, it stands as a symbol of the value of peaceful resolution of differences.

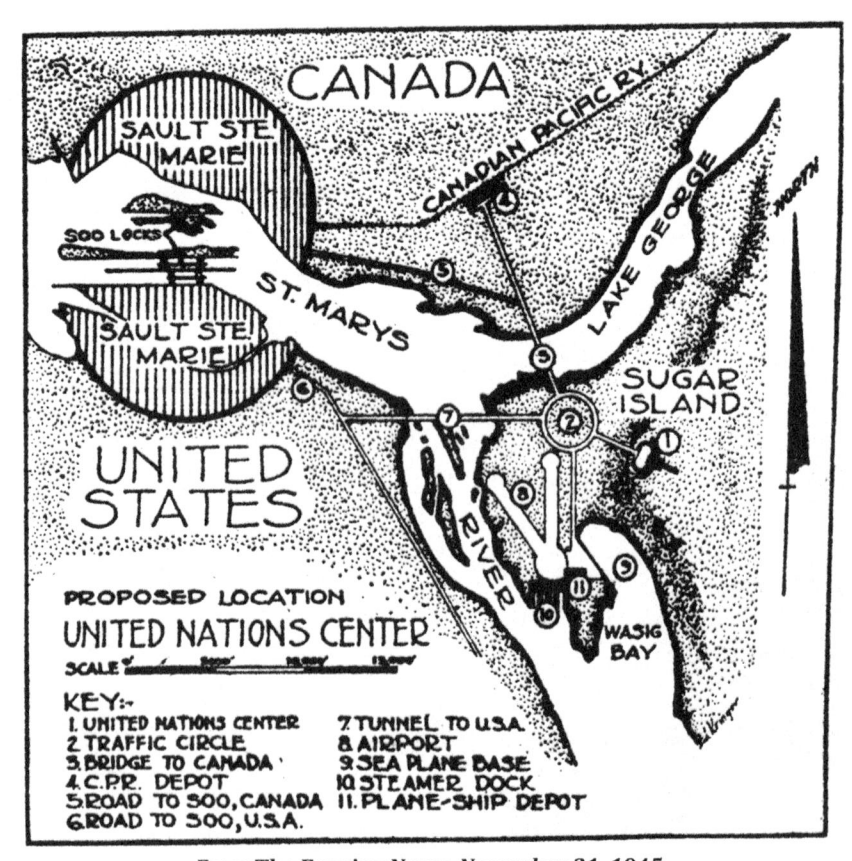

From The Evening News, *November 21, 1945.*

Maurice Hunt, Mayor of Sault Ste. Marie (Michigan) in the mid 1940s, was also a prominent figure in this effort; his scrapbook is now in the Michigan Room of the L.S.S.U. Library. The scrapbook contains numerous newspaper clippings relating to the United Nations site campaign, which may have had a "promotional" or "boosterism" aspect to it, but was a serious effort as well. Statements of support appear from many civic and service organizations, as well as newspapers from both Michigan and Ontario. A committee of 14 area citizens (none from Sugar Island, however) was formed to make the bid. Twenty-two localities in North America were making similar proposals.

Several related items are included. In the map on the previous page, Lake George has migrated several miles upstream of its current location. This figure was part of a full page advertisement published in *The Evening News* on November 21, 1945. The ad appealed to the readers, asking that they send letters of support for the Sugar Island site to the international committee charged with making the final decision concerning the headquarter's location.

Start Hearing UNO Bidders

LONDON, Dec. 1. (*P*)—A sub-committee of the United Nations Preparatory Commission today began hearing deputations from more than a score of American and Canadian cities which are offering sites for the permanent UNO headquarters.

The sub-committee — most of whose members have declared themselves in favor of establishing the headquarters in the United States—began hearing the delegations in alphabetical order, starting with Atlantic City, N. J.

Delegates from Australia, Colombia, Cuba, Egypt, Iran, The Netherlands and Yugoslavia make up the sub-committee.

In alphabetical order, Sault Ste. Marie's invitation will be next to the last to be considered. The bidders for the UNO headquarters are:
Atlantic City
Black Hills, S. D.
Champaign county, Illinois.
Chicago
Denver
Hyde Park, N. Y.
Three sites in Indiana, presently unlisted.
Miami, Fla.
The Monterey Peninsula of California.
Monticello, Va.
The Moraga Valley near San Francisco.
Navy Island at Niagara Falls, N. Y.
Newport, R. I.
New York City.
Philadelphia.
Richmond, Va.
San Francisco.
Saratoga Springs, N. Y.
International Island (Sugar Island) at Sault Ste. Marie, between the United States and Canada.
Waimanaloa, Hawaii.
The city of Quebec and Vancouver Island have issued invitations from Canada.
No formal invitations have been issued from other parts of the world.

From The Evening News, *December 2, 1945*

Note that the proposed site of the United Nations Center itself is on the high ground northeast of Baie de Wasai, about where the Vuori farm is. At the time, some were referring to the island as "International Island", apparently to strengthen the case that it was a suitable international site. Perhaps it was a far-fetched idea, but as an old friend said to me, "So was the idea of building a bridge across the Straits of Mackinac - until they actually did it!" In any case, the campaign is a piece of island history that provides a springboard for speculating - "What if Sugar Island HAD been chosen ... ?"

From **The Evening News,** *November 13, 1945*

Ice Dam in 1951

Periodically since regular ferry service was begun, island residents have been isolated from the mainland for several days at a time. The most recent occurrence prior to the publishing of this book was in the spring of 1991, when the ferry rudder was damaged during an attempt to rescue a man from the Canadian side who was out on thin ice upriver from the ferry lane.

Winter navigation has been the cause of several problems with ice blocking the ferry lanes. However, in 1951 Mother Nature cut the supply line, when severe cold and heavy snow led to an ice dam forming at Little Rapids Cut just before Christmas. The ice there was reported in an *Evening News* article dated Dec. 21, 1951, to be driven to a depth of 15 feet, and the ferry couldn't run for five days. Flooding occurred in the Sault harbor, with water levels reported to be two and one-half feet higher than normal, and the gates at the compensating dam were closed in an effort to alleviate that problem. The ferry between Sault, Michigan, and Sault, Ontario, also had to suspend operations for a time.

Flooding in the Sault harbor as a result of the ice dam at Little Rapids Cut, December, 1951 (courtesy of John Wellington).

ROUGH TRIP AHEAD! Dec. 22, 1951

Harry Holdsworth and his "Sno-Mobile" setting out for Sugar Island. The men are checking the ice with spuds and attempting to smooth it out a little *(courtesy Evening News).*

In the time-honored tradition of islanders, men were soon crossing the ice bridge near Six Mile Point to get needed groceries and supplies to their families on Sugar Island. Alex Cadreau was reportedly the first to cross, marking the trail. The ice in the channel was extremely rough; some chunks of it were standing on end to a height of three or four feet and it was not possible to pull sleighs across, so the supplies had to be carried in backpacks. By the fourth day of the ordeal, C.G. Sanderson of Sault Ste. Marie was using his private plane to conduct an airlift. The ice in Baie de Wasai was much smoother than out in the channel, so Sanderson could set his plane down in the Baie. His first run carried mail and he was met on the ice by about 50 island residents, according to an article in the Dec. 20th issue of The Evening News. He completed seven flights that day, and was involved in similar missions to the island over the years. The next day, Bay Mills Township Supervisor Harry Holdsworth used his "sno-mobile," a Model A equipped with tracks and normally used in commercial fishing on Whitefish Bay, to haul supplies and gasoline to the island. County snowplows had just about exhausted their fuel stocks by that time. Holdsworth and the men helping him managed to bring 1,000 gallons of gasoline across the ice during the crisis. Dan Boyer told me he crossed the ice to get to his home on the island Friday night, December 21. The snow was knee-deep on the ice. By the next afternoon, the dam had broken and there was a wide stretch of open water where he had crossed.

Build-A-Road Day

The first "Build-A-Road Day" was held on Sugar Island on June 17, 1950, and most of the following information has been taken from *Evening News* articles published June 16 through June 20 of that year. This event was inspired in part by old-time work bees and, of course, by the sorry state of the roads themselves. But sponsors also gave credit to the citizens of Kerrville, Texas, who had held a "Build-a-Recreation Field Day" and the story had been written up in the *Evening News*.

A group of islanders organized themselves into the Sugar Island Development Association in 1948, electing Gil Nelson as its president. This group spearheaded the road building effort and had other goals as well, such as promoting the island downstate, and attracting tourists. Mr. Nelson was general chairman of the event, and "Hobie" Norris was the "chief expediter." Other committees and their chairmen were:

Gen. Supervision & Technical Asssitance	Everett Clegg
Tools	Ed Pine
Transportation of Tools	Leo DeLisle
Signs	Esko Kaikkonen
Safety	Horace France
Night Patrol	Leo Sylvester
Housing	Mrs. Willa Wellbaum
Tickets	Fred Heller
Labor	Pete Maleport
First Aid	Frank Trombley, Sault Fire Chief
Transportation of Workers	J. T. Willis
Food	Royce Curlis
Parade	Fire Chief Trombley
Indian Liaison	James Cadreau

Working on a culvert site, probably near McIntosh Corner (the corner of Three Mile Road and Homestead Road). The six men are unidentified *(courtesy Mary Murray).*

The goal of the project was to construct five miles of road, to be done in eight hours, starting at 7 A.M. Saturday morning. In fact, work continued until early evening, and resumed Sunday morning, resulting in 10 miles of new or improved road, in the vicinity of the old Town Hall on Townline Road. Thousands of yards of gravel were spread, hills were cut down for improved safety and some clearing of brush and trees was carried out. Sixty to seventy pieces of heavy road-building equipment were involved, much of it donated by area contractors, with one piece even coming from Sault Ste. Marie, Ontario. Ironically, some equipment was stranded on the island because part of the ramp on the ferry dock was damaged. So a few crews continued working part of Monday while the ramp was repaired. (It's an ill wind ...). A total of about 500 people took part, from the island and Sault. Island women supplied food and coffee, with proceeds slated to go to an island youth organization.

Governor G. Mennen "Soapy" Williams at a Build-A-Road Day, June 17, 1950. Williams is wearing a head-dress given to him by Charley Andrews. Behind the Governor is Earl McKerchie, and possibly Gene Thibert (courtesy of Mary Murray).

A full page ad in the *Evening News*, sponsored by 84 area businesses, billed the effort as "Democracy in Action." Speaker of the Michigan House Victor Knox, Sault Mayor William Freeman and several city commissioners and county supervisors were there, as well as Michigan Governor G. Mennen Williams and State Highway Commissioner Charles Ziegler. Dan Boyer said, "Gil Nelson did a good job keeping the Democrats at one end of the project, and the Republicans at the other end".

Williams was on the island for the latter part of the day, and commended the project as "an example of what can be done when everyone cooperates to do a job." The original "Build-A-Road Day" has inspired several successors over the years.

Electricity

Cloverland Electric Company brought electrical service to Sugar Island on Dec. 21, 1953, which made it something of a Christmas present for the island. (According to National Geographic's *Historical Atlas of the United States*, in 1950, 78% of the rural dwellings in the country had electrical service, and by 1955, the figure was 95%, so the electrification of Sugar Island came later than in most parts of the country.) Prior to that time, some people had their own generators, such as the 32-volt Delco system with several rows of glass batteries that my father had, but kerosene was undoubtedly a big seller on the island until the mid-1950s. I remember the time quite well, because my dad did house-wiring as a sideline, and since I was in my mid-teens, I was the right size to climb up in an attic or into a crawl space to pull wire. I was also a general "go-fer," fetching tools, supplies and the like. "Dollar waitin' on a dime" was something I heard more than once when I dawdled a bit. But the job I dreaded most was driving the ground rod, which was a solid copper rod about six feet long that had to be driven entirely into the ground. That's when I learned practical aspects of island geology. The island is mostly rock - or so it seemed to me, at least; some of those rods must have looked like a pretzel when I finished with them. In 1991, Cloverland Electric had 630 customers on the island.

Telephone Service

Royce Curlis was quoted in the Jan. 29, 1960, issue of *The Evening News* as saying, "This is the most important thing for us since we got electricity on the island six years ago." He was talking about the installation of the first telephone on the island available to the general public. Michigan Bell had agreed to provide a telephone booth at the ferry dock if the islanders laid the cable from the mainland. Curlis heard about some cable on Neebish Island that the Coast Guard had pulled out of service and replaced, so the Township bid $113 and purchased 6,500 feet of it - some of which was not usable, how-

From left: Congressman Raymond Clevenger, Township Supervisor Royce Curlis, Richard Howard, Howard Haight, Harold Nelson from Michigan Bell Telephone Co., and Gert Wilds, owner of the Baie de Wasai Store (courtesy Evening News*).*

ever. After piecing together enough to cross the river near the ferry, Fred Heller, a retired Army officer who lived on the island, and Merlin McCoy, lifelong islander and owner of the Hilltop Bar, laid the cable. It was unwound from a large reel on the ferry, piloted by owner Ken Bonathan, who donated his time and the use of the ferry to the project.

On December 16, 1964, connections for telephone service to the Bayview Store at Baie de Wasai were completed. This was the first private telephone on the island, and soon thereafter there were 120 customers. Cloverland Electric allowed power poles to be used for the telephone lines, which enabled the service to be offered. The photograph on the previous page commemorates the first telephone call from a private telephone on the island.

Bridges

Telephone and electrical service have made the island less isolated and a more convenient place to live. It is interesting to speculate about the effects on the island's character that a bridge would have. At several times in the past, effort has been expended toward that end. The first time, in 1890, has already been mentioned in Chapter One. Later, the effort to attract the United Nations to Sugar Island contained a proposal for a tunnel from the mainland to the island, and a bridge from the northwest side of the island to Ontario.

Another time was in the mid-1950s, when the International Bridge was in its conceptual stages. John Matheson described the situation in an *Evening News* article entitled "Bridging the Saults Wasn't Easy,"published August 5, 1990, and quoted in part below with his permission:

> At the time, Gil Nelson was Mr. Sugar Island in some circles. In the final push that led to the construction of the Straits of Mackinac Bridge, Gil had coined a slogan: "Holy Mackinac - Bridge It Now." He was quite a promoter, operating from his base at his resort near Homestead on the downriver tip of Sugar Island.
>
> He was one of the regular visitors to the newspaper office, and he was always good for a lively conversation and perhaps a few lines of choice

"copy," which was one newspaper name for a story.

Well, when the discussion got serious about bridging the St. Marys River, Gil Nelson made his move. He perceived this as one opportunity to get a bridge to Sugar Island, and the push was on. His idea, in essence, was to kill two birds with one stone, with a bridge from the Michigan side to Sugar Island, and then to Ontario.

In retrospect, Gil might have had something, provided the engineering could have been worked out to accommodate the vessel traffic through the Little Rapids cut, the approaches, and all those other details. His route would probably have led to considerable development on Sugar Island (and one can argue the pros and cons of this one). But for Gil Nel-

***Gil Nelson in 1976** (photo by Bill Hamilton).*

son, opportunity was knocking, and Sugar Island never had a bigger booster...

Matheson then described the politics and business concerns that led to the selection of the bridge location, and the traffic patterns that have evolved. The article concludes as follows:

The Canadian Sault has its own traffic problems, and Sugar Island remains relatively undeveloped. This is either good or bad, depending on your point of view.

However, we're beginning to hear that the ferry may no longer be adequate to handle movement to and from the Island. Further, it would have been heavily impacted - as Gil Nelson foresaw, had the bridge to Ontario been routed to the island...

Things sure would have been different if Gil Nelson's argument had carried the day.

"Purgatory Point," Gil Nelson's resort. Among those in the picture are Gil Nelson, Senator Philip Hart, "Sonny" Eliot, and "Pud" Hamilton (courtesy Bill & Nancy Saunders).

Another of Mr. Nelson's promotional efforts is depicted in the photograph on the previous page. Nelson reasoned that since his resort at the southern end of Sugar Island was geographically somewhere between Paradise and Hell (Michigan, that is,) it could reasonably be called Purgatory Point. Detroit radio personality "Sonny" Eliot, who often gave temperatures and other news items from remote places in northern Michigan, liked the sound of Purgatory Point, donated a set of weather instruments to be placed at Nelson's, and often thereafter gave weather and fishing news from Purgatory Point.

In Conclusion

Sugar Island was an Indian Reservation for the short time period from 1836 to 1841. Soon thereafter, it attracted farmers such as the Payment families and entrepreneurs such as Philetus Church and Allen Rains, who recognized the strategic location of the island with regard to shipping in the St. Marys River.

Farming was evidently the main occupation of islanders through the late 1800's and into the 1900's as the population grew and peaked at about 700 residents in 1940. As farming declined, so did the population until 1970, when only 237 people were year round residents - virtually the same population the island had had 100 years earlier, in 1870.

A look at the population figures in the appendix of the book will show that the 30 year downward trend in population that began between 1940 and 1950 seems to have reversed itself, with a modest growth occurring in the last two decades. The census of school children from Sugar Island attending Sault Ste. Marie Public Schools reveals the same modest growth, which means young families continue to make their home on the island. The total pupil count was 61 in 1970, 74 in 1980, and 76 in 1990.

Ferry traffic figures show a much more dramatic growth. According to Eastern Upper Peninsula Transportation Authority figures, in fiscal year 1982-83, 110,000 vehicles were taken to and from Sugar Island by the ferry. For fiscal year 1989-90, that figure had increased to about 174,000, constituting an increase of 58% in eight years. A recent Michigan Department of Transportation report contained estimates of future annual ferry traffic in the year 2009-2010 which ranged from a low figure of 337,000 vehicles to a high figure of 431,000 vehicles, depending on assumptions that were made about various rates of growth. *Author's note, added in 2020*: As it turned out, the projections from the DOT were not very accurate. The actual numbers of vehicle crossings were 260,986 in 2010 and 279,178 in 2019. I suspect some—perhaps many—islanders are happy that the traffic didn't increase nearly as much as had been predicted. Incidentally, while the average annual growth in traffic was about 7% between 1982-83 and 1989-90, during the thirty-year period from 1989-90 to 2019, the average annual growth was just 1.6%.

Someone more familiar with the island might have an explanation for the big difference in growth rates, but I don't even have a guess.

The island has changed a good deal over the period of time covered in this book, but that is, of course, to be expected, since the time period covered has been about 140 years. If the traffic at the ferry is a reliable indicator, changes are probably occurring much more rapidly in our own time, making it all the more imperative that an effort be made to preserve what one can of the island's past in words, photographs and perhaps even artifacts.

It is the people who give the island so much of its character, of course. My father was fond of saying, "There's lots of time on Sugar Island." Those who knew him would agree with me when I say that he spent as much time as he possibly could on it. He built two different homes on the island—one a half-mile south of Baie de Wasai when he and my mother were newlyweds, and one near Brassar Point—meant as a retirement home—about twenty years later, after he got tired of losing docks to the ice in the shallower waters of the Baie. Although Dad got to enjoy the Brassar Point place mostly during weekends and vacations for only about fifteen years, Mom lived there for over three decades. Both homes are still standing, and both are unique in their own ways. Pete and Pearl would be pleased to know that their grandson—my contractor-son Dan Arbic—has built several very nice places on Sugar Island for clients, thus maintaining an Arbic-Island connection for third generation. And because of a couple of very tough excavations on those jobs, Dan now has a deeper knowledge of the island's rocky underpinnings than I do from my experience driving those ground-rods as a teenager so many years earlier for my dad.

Expanded Edition Samplings

As I write this in 2020, it is about thirty years since I began work on the *Sugar Island Sampler*. It holds a special place in my heart, since it was the first book I had ever written. I thought that it would be the only one, but I found that I enjoyed the research process, and the special pleasure when I uncovered interesting historical facts that were new to me—especially if I thought they would be interesting and new to anyone who might read my book. It launched an interest in local history that has become a rewarding pursuit in retirement.

Much has happened on the island, of course, since first publication of the *Sampler*. I will leave it to others to explore those changes more fully, but I decided to provide a few updates and new photos that tie in to material in the original book, or deserve special mention.

Philetus Church

In discussing the early island economy, the trading post and dock at Churchville Point was treated extensively and two photos of the property, as well as an advertisement for some of the many items he offered for sale to passing steamboats were included in the book.

The portrait of Philetus Church (on next page) was given to the Chippewa County Historical Society in 2009 by Church descendants Jennylee (Church) Olesek and Rosalee (Church) Sasso, both of whom grew up on Drummond Island, where their grandfather J. Wells Church had moved his family after leaving Sugar Island.

One of the businesses for which Church was well-known was making and selling raspberry jam. I was delighted when Mr. Jack Deo of Marquette shared the photograph below with the Chippewa County Historical Society. It shows part of the Church Trading Post, with the sign above the door making clear that jam was a major offering. We don't have a date for the image, but the year 1860 is probably not too far off.

This portrait of Philetus Church was made ca. 1835, when Mr. Church was about 25 years old. (courtesy of Jennylee (Church) Olesek and Rosalee (Church) Sasso)

In this image, it seems likely that the man in the white coat is Philetus Church. Note the firewood, ready for sale to passing steamboats. Also note the weathervane: the Churches were sailors. J. Wells Church mentioned the wind strength and direction at the beginning of every entry in his journals. Photo courtesy of Jack Deo, Superior View Historic Photography

New Bridge on the Causeway

A major project to restore fish habitat in the Little Rapids area resulted in the construction of a 660 foot bridge on the causeway. Remarkably, this $7.5 million project was completed in about five months, in the summer and early fall of 2016, under the direction of the Chippewa County Road Commission, headed by Manager Rob Laitinen. The lead contractor was the Payne & Dolan Company, based in Waukesha, Wisconsin.

In order to maintain traffic flow, contractors built a temporary diversion of the causeway around the bridge location, on the north side, as shown in the image below. During the planning phase, input from Sugar Island residents was influential in the decision to construct the temporary roadway to allow for two-way traffic at all times. The base for the diversion was built with about 66,000 cubic yards of stone donated by the U.S. Army Corps of Engineers from the early 20th century Neebish Rock Cut excavation. After the new bridge opened for traffic, the diversion was removed and the stones were hauled to the county gravel pit on the island, to be crushed for gravel as needed on island roads—a nice additional benefit of the project for island roads. The sidewalk and railing on the south side of the bridge, which allows for fishing as well as pedestrian traffic, was also a result of local input.

Support for the roadway on the bridge is provided by 30 huge precast concrete girders that are 125 feet long, and almost five feet tall. Six girders were needed for each span, and there are five spans on the bridge. The girders were manufactured in Manitowoc, Wisconsin, and brought here by a barge. The barge was then tied up to the ferry dock, and the girders were transferred to special trucks. This was done over two nights, so normal ferry traffic was almost unaffected. Each of the girders weighs about 52 tons; it required two large cranes to place each of them on the support piers.

This satellite image from GoogleEarth was taken July 12, 2016. The five horseshoe-shaped regions are where the pilings that support the bridge will be constructed. The thin light-colored lines both on the north and south sides of the construction site are containment "curtains," meant to reduce the spread of turbidity from the site.   *Courtesy of Google Earth*

This view is looking southwest, as one of the huge girders is being lowered into place. The size of the girder is apparent by noting that it is almost as tall as the worker in the image. Courtesy of the Chippewa County Road Commission

After the new bridge opened for traffic, the temporary roadway was removed. In about two days, a fleet of 18 large dump trucks such as shown here transported the boulders that were used to form the base of the roadway to the County Gravel Pit off Three Mile Road on the island. Courtesy of The Walbec Group / Payne & Dolan, Inc. of Waukesha, Wisconsin

Just in the author's lifetime, there have been three different provisions designed to allow water flow through the causeway. The photo on page 65 shows two of the three wooden bridges that I remember as a youngster in the 1950s. They were replaced, probably in the 1970s, by two culverts six feet in diameter. Those culverts were then removed in 2016, when the new bridge was built. I contacted the Great Lakes Hydraulics and Hydrology Office of the Detroit District of the U.S. Army Corps of Engineers, to inquire about the flow through the causeway before and after the bridge was built. According to their measurements, the amount of water flowing under the bridge from the north side of the causeway to the south side, compared to the amount that formerly flowed through the culverts, is anywhere from ten times as much during high-water conditions, to perhaps twenty times as much during low water conditions. The increased flow has changed a silt bottom in that area to cobble, which provides more suitable spawning conditions for several species of fish and a better habitat for invertebrate life. As a matter of separate interest, anywhere from one percent to three percent of the total flow of the St. Marys River passes under the causeway bridge, with a higher percentage occurring during high water conditions.

Publication of *Big John* and re-printing of *Joe Pete*

Ms. Florence McClinchey and her 1929 book *Joe Pete* were discussed beginning on page 93. While researching for that part of the book in 1990, I met Ms. McClinchey's sister-in-law Mary McClinchey, and Mary's daughter Sue Anderson. Ms. Anderson lives in Oklahoma, but visits the Sault most summers. She told me that she had a manuscript copy of an unpublished sequel to *Joe Pete* that her aunt Florence had been working on at the time of her death; the sequel was entitled *Big John*. Sue brought the manuscript with her the next summer when she visited again. She let me read the story, and I asked if she would consider publishing it. Happily, it has recently been published through the efforts of Ms. Anderson, and Mr. Phil Bellfy. One of the more interesting features of *Big John* is that each chapter begins with a symbol or icon that we are told represented something to the Ojibwe or Anishinabe of Sugar Island, and probably much more broadly. Florence came to know Sugar Island's Native American community well. The symbols were collected both by Florence

Symbol of Mystical Power   Symbol of Sociability

Two of about twenty symbols from **Big John**

***The reprint of* Joe Pete *and first publication of* Big John *by Ziibi Press, Sault Ste. Marie, Michigan.** *Photo by the author*

herself, and by Father William Gagnieur, who worked for years with Native Americans in the Upper Peninsula, so I believe that they are very likely to be authentic. Some of them were also reported by Henry Schoolcraft. The image on the previous page shows two of the symbols that I especially liked. More of the symbols can be seen on the cover of *Big John*, also on the previous page.

Mr. Bellfy took the lead in the publication of *Big John* and the reprinting of *Joe Pete*, and acted as editor for both books. As a Native American himself, he wrote these words in an Editor's Postscript to *Big John*, regarding the very mixed reception that *Joe Pete* received locally when it was published, and the possibility of the same kind of reception for *Big John*:

> *Joe Pete* was published nearly 90 years ago; *Big John* was written over 70 years ago. During this period, and for centuries before, Native People suffered almost unimaginable deprivations across the entire Hemisphere—and it makes people uncomfortable to read these two novels as Florence McClinchey exposes the cultural, psychic, and physical wounds of those deprivations.
>
> The "Indian New Deal," instituted under the Roosevelt Administration, did alleviate the suffering of American Indians to some degree, but, as McClinchey revealed in both her novels, the situation of many, if not most, American Indians remained dire. In summary, this was the period during which the "Indians-as-a-Vanishing-Race" ideology was the dominant sentiment of even the most sympathetic observer.
>
> So, yes, many readers are disturbed by the revelations of both *Joe Pete* and *Big John*, but, nevertheless, there are also many, including this Editor, who feel that it is better to confront the realities of the American Indian experience, both historical and contemporary, no matter how painful, than to suppress or ignore that grim reality. Both of these masterful novels give the reader a glimpse of that reality.

This picture of Florence McClinchey and her brother Allen McClinchey was probably taken around 1940. Florence's cabin is in the background. Photo courtesy of Florence's niece, Sue Anderson

Nicolas Bellin's Map Showing Isle St. Georges

One of the changes in this printing that I am most excited about is the inclusion of a map from 1744 by the French cartographer Nicolas Bellin. It is a beautiful piece of work, and I have extracted a portion of it to use on the back cover of this printing. I am including the entire map here, although it loses some of its loveliness when it is not rendered in color. Whitefish Point is just visible at the upper left edge of the map displayed here, and it is denoted "Pointe au Poisson Blanc," which literally translates to "Whitefish Point." I was surprised to learn that, as early as 1744, the point was already known by its modern name. I suppose there is a possibility that the name was added later to the map, but I am taking it at face value. Another surprise for me was that Lime Island was denoted "Isle au Plâtre," which is, literally, "Plaster (lime) Island." But the main reason that I wanted to display this map is that it shows that the French of the mid-eighteenth century knew our Sugar Island as "Isle St. Georges," or St. George Island. The modern echo of that is, of course, that we still call the lake on the east side of the island Lake George. Apparently,

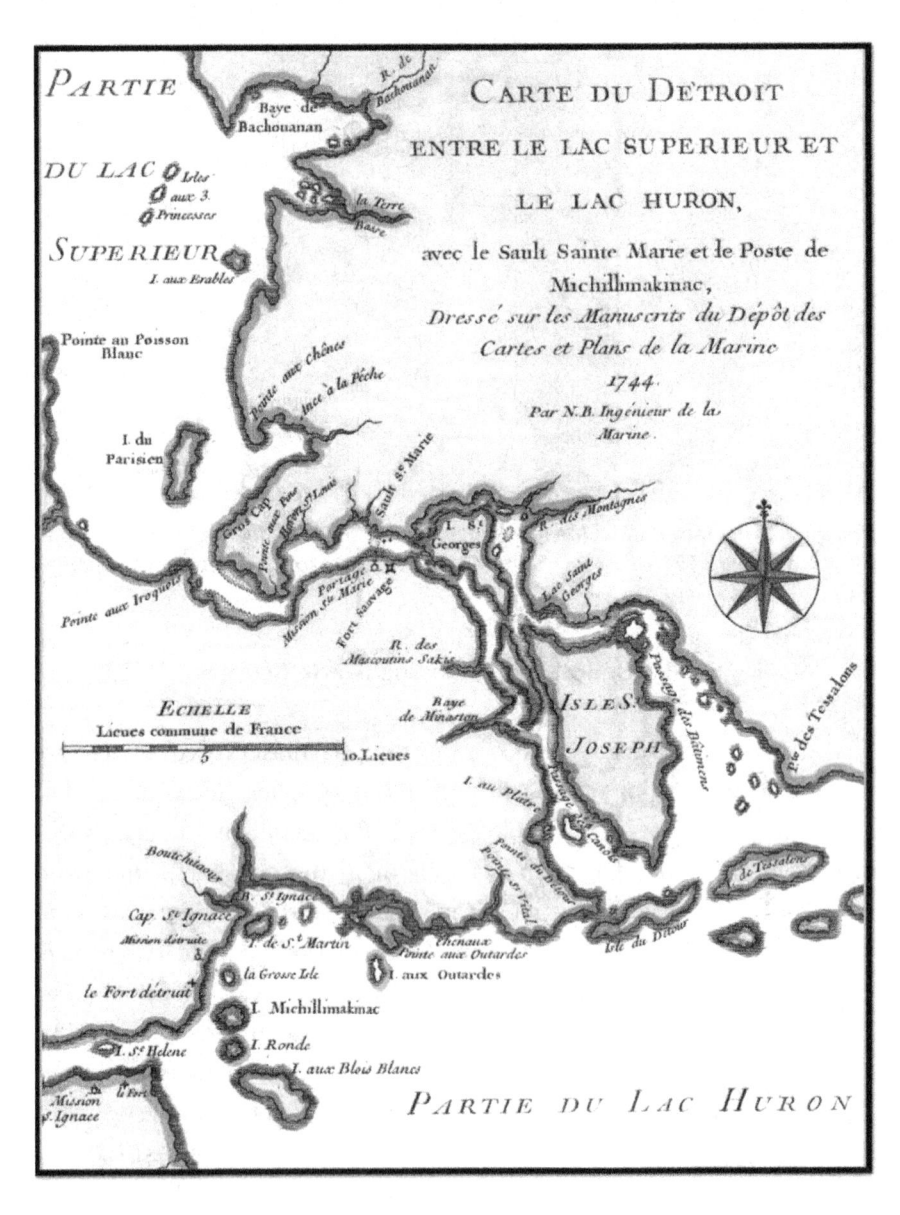

French cartographer Nicolas Bellin's "Map of the Strait Between Lake Superior and Lake Huron" from 1744. Although the shape of Sugar Island is unmistakable, Neebish Island and Drummond Island need some adjustments. (courtesy of Barry Lawrence Ruderman Antique Maps, www.RareMaps.com)

Monsieur Bellin was never in this area; he made the map based on drawings and notes filed in French naval records. An eight by ten inch full-color print of the map, suitable for framing, can be purchased from the Chippewa County Historical Society.

Sugar Island Historical Preservation Society

One of the new institutions on Sugar Island—born since this book was first published—is the Sugar Island Historical Preservation Society (SIHPS). A group of seventeen people got together at Studebaker's Restaurant in the Sault in February, 2001 to discuss the possible formation of a society to be focused on historical matters on the island. The people who attended that first meeting were: George Snider, Yvonne and Ron Peer, George Albrecht, Fr. Ted Brodeur, Sue Schacher, Joe and Rose Menard, Kim Gravelle, Joan King Corbiere, Pearl Menard, Wayne Corbiere, Sandra Reining, Leo Rich, Holly Kibble, and Cathy Abramson. After several informal meetings, the group organized formally and now has IRS 501 (c) 3 designation as a non-profit group. One of its first major projects involved the Holy Angels Church in Payment. For many years, Al and Pearl Menard and their family had helped to maintain the church, which had been built in the 1850s by Michael Payment under the supervision of Bishop Frederic Baraga. By the time SIHPS came into existence, the building needed to be raised and stabilized. Eventually, interested individuals and SIHPS working together succeeded in putting the church on a new foundation, and giving it a new roof as well as a fresh coat of paint. Burt Menard and his father Joe deserve recognition for a new metal cross atop the steeple, crafted through Burt's efforts, and installed by Joe. The original wooden cross had long since disappeared. The church was recently visited by group of Slovenian Canadians (Baraga was Slovenian) on a bus tour of Upper Peninsula sites related to Bishop Baraga.

A second major accomplishment was the acquisition of the Finn Hall at Willwalk on Homestead Road. The hall was the center of social life among the Finnish islanders for a few decades after it was built in the mid-1920s. Old photographs document use by the entire island community for special occasions. It had fallen into serious disrepair during the latter part of the twentieth century, and was donated to SIHPS by owner Duane "Dewey" Carlson in 2005.

The group ran many fund-raisers, received a grant from the Finlandia Society, and worked for several years restoring it with volunteer labor. The project required relocating the porcupine that behaved as though it owned the building and looked down at the crew from the rafters. A new metal roof, rolled asphalt siding, re-glazed windows and painted trim brought the exterior back to life. The tin ceiling, water damaged with jagged rusty holes was expertly repaired by Art Leighton. The famous maple dance floor, retaining some evidence of chewing by the porcupine, was patched and renewed by Jim Pim and others. The dedicated carpentry crew included; Reino Syrjala (titular supervisor), Al Swanson, Dave Bean, Karl Kirn and Bernie Roy. The stage area was jacked up and re-supported and missing floor boards were replaced. Stage curtains and back drop were sewn by Pat Kirn and Linda Sumner. On the grounds, a first-rate privy was built, and the property is now known as the History Center.

The hall is one of the oldest surviving examples of the many Finnish Halls that were built across the northern U.S. and Canada. It was re-dedicated to the people of Sugar Island in 2010, and since then has been used for many events, including public meetings sponsored by SIHPS, musical presentations, and the annual All-Island Community Yard Sale, a fund-raiser for the organization. The society is also supported by proceeds from an annual quilt raffle. Over the years many hands have contributed to designing, piecing and quilting, with notably beautiful results. Some of the many craftswomen, looking back to Sylvia Hovey, include Barbara Hinton, Pat Kirn, and Magaret and Adrienne Beckham. Out of town donors of two quilts are Pam Moore and Eila Mathias, who have long-standing connections to Sugar Island.

A one-of-a-kind raffle was made possible by the refurbishment of a donated 1970s Mercury Marquis station wagon. Art Leighton restored its original beauty and function, set a lounging gorilla on the hood for attention and displayed it at various U.P. events one summer, inspiring willingness to take a chance.

A third major preservation task began when SIHPS acquired Brassar School, donated by Paul Juhala. A hired crew moved it to the History Center from the Juhala farm on Hay Point Road. (Before its use as a farm outbuilding, it was located at the corner of N. Brassar and Seppi Roads.) This was a challenging job, since the roof had to be removed in one piece for transport and then be reinstalled after the school had been placed on its new foundation.

The Franks family and the Jarl Hiltunen estate, through trustee Kathy Cairns, made this phase possible. The completed project will present a Sugar Island school to the public (the last of five that served over many years), have space for an office and permit the display of the growing collection of donated Sugar Island artifacts and memorabilia.

Another building at the History Center is the Hiltunen family sauna, donated by the Jarl Hiltunen Estate. Quoting from SIHPS notes, the sauna "... is a fine representative of the vital element of the lives of many Finnish and non-Finnish Sugar Island families." Author's note: we had a sauna at our cabin south of Baie de Wasai, built out at the end of a "dike," so we could take a steam-bath, and then jump in the river.

The society welcomes participation in its activities, including an oral history project, local historical research, and care of the growing collection of artifacts and documents. The group deserves a huge pat on the back for their hard work and ambitious goals. The current president is George Snider—who was also the president for the first ten years of the society's existence. Other members of the Board of Directors are: Kim Gravelle, Vice President, Gayle Belleau, Treasurer, Anita McKerchie, Secretary, and Trustees Wayne Corbiere, Sharon Mustonen, and Pat Kirn. Two members should be thanked for steadfast interest in SIHPS. Aili Allen has inspired some of the memorial donors, has been hostess to many visitors, as well as telling the story of the Finnish chapter on Sugar Island. Bernard Roy, a keeper of traditional knowledge, is mysteriously able to solve problems because he enjoys the trust of everybody.

The Finn Hall in 2005 as acquired by SIHPS. Photo by Allan Swanson

After restoration, ca. 2007. Courtesy of Allan Swanson

W. P. A. Project

A little-known activity near the end of the Great Depression was a project that was set up on Sugar Island by the Works Progress Administration. It was designed to provide employment for some of the island's Native Americans, and to promote the preservation of some of their traditional skills, such as basket-weaving, making snowshoes, and making birchbark articles. In addition, a large amount of handmade rustic furniture was manufactured; much of it was purchased by the Michigan Department of Conservation for use in some of its facilities. Some of the furniture also was purchased for the Chase S. Osborn Preserve on the island. In May of 1940, there was an open house held at the Finn Hall—adjacent to where the work was carried out—to display examples of the many items produced. Afterward, some of the items were displayed in a show-window at the Hub Department Store in the Sault, as shown in the photo on the next page.

This display was in the window of The Hub Department Store during the summer of 1940. Several baskets, a landing net, a snowshoe frame, and a very graceful fishing creel can be seen. Courtesy of the Gordon Daun Collection, Chippewa County Historical Society

FINNISH HALL — **Willwalk Sugar Island**

All Day Display of Indian-Handicraft Production
Evening Program 7:30 P. M.
Old Fashioned Box Social Not to Exceed 25¢ per Lunch

SPEAKERS	PROJECT NO. 8421-S-181
Township Officials	Sugar Island Unit
PROGRAM	PROJECT WORKERS

Program	Project Workers	
The Smoking of Pipe of Peace	Jennie Williams	Elmer Sprinkett
Peace Pipe Dance	Issac Marshall	Peter J Frechette
Telling of a Little Joke	Robert Thorne	Walter Gurnoe
Scalp Dance	Joseph Johndro w	Joseph Andrews
Indian Love Song	Joseph Gurnoe	William J. Riley
Bridal Dance	Peter Causley	Edward Gurnoe
Papakiwis Dance	John Nolan	Samuel Williams
Snake Dance	Robert Mendoskin	Paul Joseph
Indian Love Song	Louis Hatch Jr.	Angeline Williams
Indian War Dance	Angeline Cadreau	John Piquette
	Roy E. Boully	Joseph S. McKerchie
Issac Marshall	Peter Joseph	Peter Pine
Director of Entertainment	Lavina Marshall	Gilbert Joseph

Proceeds to go to Local Sponsors

This invitation to an Open House in May, 1940, at the Finn Hall was printed on birchbark. There were 26 islanders who worked on the project. The project apparently attracted quite a few visitors over the year or so that it was in operation.
Courtesy of Chippewa County Historical Society

The picture below shows that the art of basket-making survives on Sugar Island, eighty years after the WPA Project. Bernadette and Roger Azevedo actually learned the craft from Nelson and Ruby Shinos, of Manitoulin Island, in the 1970s. Roger starts with a black ash log, removes the bark, pounds it to loosen the layers, splits the layers into thin splints, and scrapes the rough side smooth. Bernadette uses this material to create her lovely baskets. It is fitting to note that Bernadette's grandmother, Jennie Williams, and her grandfather Louis Hatch are among the workers listed on the WPA invitation shown on the previous page.

For many years in the 20th century, *The Evening News* included occasional news summaries from small settlements in the area. I'm not sure when the practice was discontinued. Probably not many today could describe where such places as Larch, Gladys, Hansenville, Mackville, Fairview or Sunshine were located. Roughly weekly, newsy items from Sugar Island settlements appeared, and I present three from May of 1940—not quite randomly selected, since one of them involves my family. I was about five months old when our family visit, noted at the bottom of the Brassar submission, occurred. Check out the score of the ballgame in the Brassar segment as well. The Brassar team must have had some sluggers. The Edison team probably refers to a team from the Edison School, which was located on Townhall Road just north of where it intersects with LaCoy Road.

BRASSAR

Quite a few women from here attended the Achievement Day at Pickford Friday, May 17. Those who attended were Mrs. Donald McFarlane, Mrs. Ernest Adams and Mrs. Joe Leask.

James Stephenson, who was employed on the Sugar Island ferry, is away working on a government boat.

Mrs. Lynn Cairns was a Sault caller Saturday.

The Brassar softball team played with the Edison team on Friday. The score was 32 to 14 in favor of Brassar.

Mrs. Ernest Adams was a Sault shopper Saturday.

The Brassar school closed Tuesday, May 21st. A picnic was given on the school grounds.

Miss Leona Leask visited at the home of Mrs. Tom Fournier at Frog Bay Monday.

Mr. and Mrs. Lynn Fox, who spent the winter months at the Sault, returned to their home here.

A number of young folks from here attended a show at the Sault on Wednesday evening.

Mr. and Mrs. Pete Arbic and family of Baie de Wasai spent Sunday at the home of Mr. and Mrs. Donald McFarlane.

I combined two different Brassar clips, to include especially interesting items, and I condensed the other two clips for reasons of space—but all items appeared as shown. Courtesy of The Evening News and Chippewa County Historical Society

PAYMENT

Emma Kabatek, Berniece Weber and a friend motored here from Menominee to get Ann Kabatek, who has been teaching the Payment school. They left for home on Sunday afternoon.

A delightful picnic lunch was held in the school on Saturday on account of rain. Songs by the pupils were enjoyed by the parents. Later the races took place and lunch was served at 5 o'clock.

Mrs. Nelson Levine of the Sault, Sam Perry of Neebish and his daughter, Mabel, of California, visited Mr. and Mrs. Angus McCoy on Sunday.

Mr. and Mrs. Joe Myotte and family of Ridge Road, Sault, visited relatives here on Sunday.

Mrs. Edwards, Paul Edwards, and Mrs. Dan Williams were business callers in Wilwalk on Sunday.

Kenneth Fox and Reino Sryjala of Brassar called here on Saturday evening.

BAIE DE WASAI

Mr. and Mrs. Orchard and family of Willwalk called at the Thibert home Saturday.

The Edison and Harding schools held their school picnic in the McIntosh grove Friday.

Mr. and Mrs. Ben Currie and Mr. and Mrs. Clyde Vowels motored to Eckerman Sunday.

Gerard Roy and Louis Perry of the Sault called here Monday. Brassar Sunday.

I asked Connie Pim, a former president of the SIHPS if she would reflect on the changes that have taken place on the island over the many years she has known and loved it. She kindly agreed to do that, in the form of a letter to you, the reader of this book. It is an engaging and lyrical description of experiencing Sugar Island first-hand, and it seems like a perfect way to end the book.

The Ferry Grandmother

To readers of Bernie's book, a valued sampler of old time sweet and rugged Sugar Island life, comes a message from a ferry grandmother waiting to cross the St. Marys River from the island to Clyde's Drive In and the rest of the world. Ready to leave our moated community, the enforced idleness can be a time bonus like a snow day. Of course, having a job or health appointment in mind, some do not enjoy the time offered for making plans, walking the dog, greeting neighbors, talking on the phone and snoozing. In those otherwise lost minutes, there are fish to look at, treading water in the river current near huge boulders. Sometimes there are American eagles in the sky, routinely patrolling the national border.

A report of life in the fast and sometimes slow lanes from the Hilltop Bar to the ferry shows how the past and present collide on Sugar Island every day. Recently, a locally rare moose was a traffic casualty in early morning foggy conditions on the hill. That was near the place chosen by a mother bear and two cubs for their successful crossing. Down on the flat and swampy section, a beaver was hit, moving from one side of its neighborhood to the other across the road. For years, a representative kingfisher has balanced on causeway wires and branches, watching over traffic and minnows below. It could have seen, and flown away from, a cluster of emergency vehicles on the splendid new causeway. When the rescue workers allowed the ordinary traffic to go through, a passenger vehicle was revealed to be resting on its roof, mid-road, like an awkward overturned turtle, empty of its unharmed people.

While nature persists on Sugar Island, visiting wildlife, also known as "folks from away," can be more surprising. A young woman, trudging inland from the ferry, asked for directions to the Hilltop, a destination on her list of visiting every country bar in the U. P. She was saved a long walk when she heard that the Hilltop (now under new ownership) was closed at that time in one of its near-death episodes.

Another visitor was not so easy to placate. She energetically wanted to know where to find Sugar Island's waterfall, holding up some printed proof. Misled by an online map, she learned that Kinsmen Park was over there in the distant hills of Sault Ste. Marie, Ontario. Vexed, she exclaimed, "Who would give two cities the same name!"

All Sugar Island residents learn that they have relatives in common. The almost-persons are: the St. Marys River; Mother Superior, the weather-making lake just over the horizon; and Old Man Winter. They support conversation in families and among strangers, representing danger and beauty on the cutting edge of a cold climate. We pause to remember loved ones affected and even lost, whether old timers or newcomers. Recently, young trees bowed down and old ones snapped in a January ice storm that left the island and the people powerless for days. Today's stories of mutual rescue and generosity and coping will be added to local historical lore, connecting us to yesteryear's farm families, town workers, lumbermen, hunters, priests, teachers, ferrymen and hundreds of children who got to school however they could.

The end of mud season is celebrated, or at least noted, by every Sugar Islander trying to keep floors clean. It coincides with maple syrup production, a traditional activity of local families and hobbyists. It starts when snow is still on the ground and lasts through the period of cold nights and warmer days as the sap rises in the trees of the sugar bush. Some tracts of maples to tap have stayed in family ownership for generations.

Although, in most years, Sugar Island provides a spectacular autumn display of bright and glowing leaves, the favorite color season can be spring. From a distance, each hill, dominated by a certain type of tree, wears the accumulated tint of buds and opening leaves. These are gentle, dusty hues of light maple red, rusty oak brown, or willow and tamarack chartreuse, accented by the near-black of dormant conifers. Marsh marigolds cover the ground in soggy zones with the chrome yellow color of a washed school bus. White Dutchman's breeches, only four inches tall, light up the ground under hardwoods for two chilly weeks before they lose the sun to leafed-out trees. That is also when the sweet-scented pale pink trailing arbutus creeps its endangered self along the sandy edge of Homestead Road.

Sugar Island is a huge pile of rock, clay, sand and gravel that has hardly changed in recent centuries. There are still quiet mature woodlands, where shafts of sunlight pass through many levels of green before almost reaching the ground. Enormous boulders, abandoned by the last glacier, are scattered about and meadows linger open many decades after agricultural disuse. Affordable or inherited open space draws people who enjoy hunting, fishing, off-road recreation and camping, in spite of the loved and hated obstacle of the ferry, a real budget-breaker in both time and money.

Now the roadsides have been cleared and mowed. In 2005, Allan Swanson chronicled the development of all-season roads on the island, which he saw as the existential challenge of the twentieth century (*Sokeri Saari: The Finnish Community on Sugar Island*). Nevertheless, he decried the mowing of the road margins. "Looks like a suburb," he said. "Where have the raspberries gone, even if they were dusty?"

More trucks rumble along the roads nowadays, heavy with logs, landscape rocks, sand and gravel. They are headed to the mainland, competing with the locals for ferry space. Letters of solicitation for timber sale have been received by land owners. Remoteness and quiet shade and wildlife habitat are being taken away a tree at a time, in one opinion. Others see income and prosperity in the activity. Emerald ash borers have already sealed the fate of many lowland ash groves. It might be a jungle out there, as Sugar Islanders learn that invasive species can quickly come right into the heart of life with significant change. For Bernadette Boushor Azevedo, a master of traditional black-ash basketry and a bearer of culture, the emerald ash borer has wiped out the material of her craft. Her husband, Roger, has prepared the weaving strips from ash logs. Is there a substitute available in this adjustment from past to future?

A notable change in island living has been the seventy-year decline in the number of family-owned fishing resorts dotting the shore all around. Signboards have come down as the properties have gone into private use with new individual or group owners. Rustic accommodation often included a boat and motor. There sometimes was a small store and a sauna. Judy Skowronek describes her parents' seasonal resort and the quiet, remote environment at Willwalk. That inspired her return to the island in retirement, long after the resort had been closed. Some new waterfront and inland homes, resorts in themselves, are built on a generous scale for year-round use by extended families. Construction is often done by Sugar Island contractors and skilled craftsmen. Such home comfort and prosperity were beyond the imagination of 1930's islanders, when private citizens loaned funds to Sugar Island Township. During the Great Depression, there was widespread inability to pay taxes. Some, however, came back to family on the island for refuge.

There are many answers to the universal conversation opener, "How did you learn about Sugar Island?" A multiple choice checklist includes: I was lost; I visit all islands; Uncle Sam sent me to the Sault; My grandparents had a farm; We stayed at the same fishing resort every summer; I used to sell worms to the resorts; We bought the Hilltop Bar; Birdwatching and sunset observing are my sports; I hunt; I was born here; I like to live on the border I am patrolling; I delivered mail. The list goes on into absurdity and privacy. The truth will not be known how this beautiful uncrowded place can exist so close to a big town. Credit and blame the ferry.

There is a story of continuity in the sale of Paul Juhala's family farm to Jeff and Rebecca Franks. Before retiring, Paul shared his knowledge of climate and sheep raising with his younger neighbors. It is gratifying to know that an old-time farmer had an interested and helpful couple ready to take over. Today there are several other farms in the island's northern cleared areas where hay fields and pastures retain the appearance of a previous century. Sandhill cranes walk and squawk in the same spacious fields used by beef cattle. Spruce grouse roost placidly in fenceline trees, spruce, of course. Other landowners care for horses, chickens, pigs and at least one donkey. At scattered hobby farms live miniature horses, goats and dogs.

A sense of well-being accompanies the return to Sugar Island after time away. It is renewing and inspiring to feel the utter calm of a summer morning on the river. By afternoon, see the racing whitecaps and scudding clouds brought by the northwest wind from Mother Superior. Memory is commonly shared of the sweet, airy call of the white-throated sparrow, flavoring a walk in the woods. For Bernie Arbic, as well, it is the "cabin bird" of childhood. His family called it "Carol's bird," after his older sister, because when she was little more than a toddler, she delighted in its call. Not to admit mosquitoes into consideration, the least favorite destroyer of any good mood is the ground hornet. Memories of a barefoot misstep are also part of returning to Sugar Island. After months elsewhere, notice the abandoned structures that have surrendered to snow load, becoming shelter for fox and raccoon, chewed on by porcupine, and explored by red squirrel, skunk and grandchild. Learn who has newly discovered Sugar Island, who is preparing a building site, and who has to leave….three more stories already.

The Ferry Grandmother

Some Facts About Sugar Island

Population, 1990 - 441
Area - 47.9 square miles, or about 30,600 acres
Length of shoreline - About 51 miles
Highest Elevation - 891 feet above sea level (about 250 feet above St. Marys River)
Assessed valuation, 1990
    1,275 residential parcels valued at $8,374,449
    18 commercial parcels valued at $518,250
Assessed valuation, 2019
    1,419 parcels valued at $52,144,900
    37 parcels were classified as "qualified agricultural"

Population Figures

Year	Sugar Island	Chippewa County
1850	?	898
1860	240	1,603
1870	238	1,689
1880	544	5,248
1890	563	12,019
1900	540	21,338
1910	625	24,472
1920	630	24,818
1930	576	25,047
1940	699	27,807
1950	447	29,206
1960	300	32,655
1970	237	32,412
1980	400	29,029
1990	441	34,604
2000	683	38,543
2010	653	38,520

Partial List of Township Supervisors

Year(s)	Supervisor
1857-1861	Philetus S. Church
1861-1862	William Palmer
1862-1868	William Wilson
1868-1880	Philetus S. Church

1880-1889	John Roussain
1889-1890	Robert Johnson
1890-1891	R.D. Bryers
1891-1895	Allen Rains
1895-1896	Charles McMahon
1896-1899	Allen Rains
1901-1914	Daniel McCoy
1915-1916	Charles McMahon
1918-1919	Wilfred Roy
1919-1923	Frank Aaltonen
1924-1925	William Walker
1926-1928	Frank Aaltonen
1929-	Dan McCoy
1929-1933	Charles McMahon
1934-	Leo Sylvester
1935-	Charles McMahon
1936-	Wilfred Roy
1937-	Leo Sylvester
1938-1944	William Murray
1945-1953	Leo Sylvester
1953-1960	Edward Saari
1960-1969	Royce Curlis
1969-1972	Paul Ecklund
1972-1976	Jon Morley
1976-1980	Jack Holt
1980-1988	Marvin Willis
1988-1992	John N. Harrington
1992-1996	Harold Mohr
1996-2000	Michael Patton
2000-2008	Derek Myerscough
2008-2016	Eric McKerchie
2016-present	Rick Roy

References

Ashley, Kathryne Belden, *Islands of the Manitou*, Crystal Bay Publishing, Coral Gables, Florida, 1978

Bayliss, Joseph E, Bayliss, Estelle L, & Milo Quaife *The River of Destiny*, Wayne University Press, Detroit, 1955

Bayliss, Joseph E. and Bayliss, Estelle L., *Historic St. Joseph Island*, Torch Press, Cedar Rapids, Iowa, 1938

Blois, John T., *Gazetteer of the State of Michigan*, Sydney L. Rood & Co., Detroit, 1839

Careless, J.M.S., *The Canadians, 1867 - 1967*, Macmillan of Canada, Toronto, 1967

Delafield, Joseph, *The Unfortified Boundary*, privately published, New York, 1943

Densmore, Frances, *Uses of Plants by the Chippewa Indians*, U.S. Government Printing Office, Washington, D.C., 1928

Dept. of Commerce, *U.S. Coast Pilot*, U.S. Department of Commerce, Washington, D.C., 1991

Fowle, Otto, *Sault Ste. Marie and Its Great Waterway*, G. P. Putnam & Sons, New York, 1925

Garrett, Wilbur E., *Historical Atlas of the United States*, National Geographic Society, Washington, D.C., 1988

Henshaw, H.W., "Indian Origin of Maple Sugar", *The American Anthropologist*, Vol. Ill, October, 1890

Hokkanen, Lawrence and Sylvia, *Karelia: A Finnish-American Couple in Stalin's Russia, 1934-1941*, North Star Press of St. Cloud, 1991

Kappler, Charles J., *Indian Treaties, 1778 - 1883*, Interland Publishers, New York, 1972

Larson, John W., *Essayons: A History of the Detroit District,* U.S. Army Corps of Engineers, U.S. Army Corps of Engineers, Detroit, 1981

McClinchey, Florence E., *Joe Pete*, Henry Holt & Co., New York, 1929

Michigan Department of State, *Statistics of Michigan, 1870*, Lansing, 1873

Moore, Charles, ed., *The Saint Marys Falls Canal: Exercises at the Semi-Centennial Celebration*, Semi-Centennial Commission, Detroit, 1907

Osborn, Stella Brunt, ed., *An Accolade for Chase S. Osborn*, City of Sault Ste. Marie, Sault Ste. Marie, Michigan, 1940

Payment, Susan, *The Geneology of the Payment Family*, privately published, Agincourt, Ontario, 1987

Pitezel, John H., *Lights and Shades of Missionary Life*, Western Books, Cincinnati, 1859

Puddefoot, W.G., *The Minute Man on the Frontier,* Thomas Y. Crowell & Co., Boston, 1895

Rezek, A. I., *History of the Diocese of Sault Ste. Marie and Marquette,* Houghton, Michigan, 1906

Romig, Walter, *Michigan Place Names*, Walter Romig, Grosse Pointe, Michigan, n.d.

Sauer, William C., *The Illustrated Atlas of Sault Ste. Marie, Michigan and Ontario*, Wm. C. Sauer, Detroit, 1888

Schoolcraft, Henry R., *History, Condition, and Prospects of the Indian Tribes of the United States, Part II*, Lippincott, Philadelphia, 1852

Taylor, William J., *Upper Michigan Postal History and Postmarks,* The Depot, Lake Grove, Oregon, 1988

Walling, Regis M., and Rupp, Rev. N. Daniel, eds. *The Diary of Bishop Frederic Baraga,* Wayne State University Press, Detroit, 1990

Wiley, Helen Seymour, *A History of the Cabin*, privately published, 1971

Micro Film Sources

U.S. Census Records for Chippewa County, 1850, 1860, 1870, 1880, 1890, 1900

Bureau of Indian Affairs Correspondence, Sault Ste. Marie Agency, 1820 - 1842 and 1842 -1852

Index

A
Aaltonen, Frank, 85, 87, 173
Abel, Mary, 104
Abramson, Cathy, 157
Adams, George, 60
Adams, George W., 22
Adams, John, 125
Adams, Margaret (photo), 94
Adams, Nellie (photo), 94
Aitken, David, 42
Albrecht, George, 157
Aloha, 37
Anderson, Sue, 14, 152, 155
Andrews family, 14, 77
Andrews, Charley, 127, (photo) 128, 137
Andrews, Ed, 129
Andrews, Joe, 41, 128
Andrews, Josephine, 128
Andrews, Pauline, 129
Arbic, Dan, 145
Arbic, Joel, 128
Arbic, Pearl, 104, (photo) 94, 145
Arbic, Pete, 103-105, 125, 145
Atkins, Alex, 39, 40, 49, 54, 97, 119
Atkins, Leslie, 39, 48, 51, 54, 114
Azevedo, Bernadette, 165, 169
Azevedo, Roger, 165, 169

B
Baie de Wasai, 39, 48, 49, 52, 79, 87, 99, 102-104, 111, 114-116, 119, 123, 125, 132, 135, 139, 159
   Post Office, 97
   store, 140, (photo) 121
   school paper, 69, 119
Bailey, George, 95
Baraga, Bishop Frederic, 79, 111, 112, 114, 116, 157, 175
Bayfield, Lt. Henry, 18, 19, 27
Beaver (photo) 59, 61
Beecroft, Bob, 111
Bell, W.J., 23, 24, 31, 81, 82
Belleau, Ed, 124
Bellfy, Phil, 14, 152, 154
Bellin, Nicolas, 155-157
Bertie, 28, 29
Big John (book) 93, 95, 152-154
Bonathan, Kenneth, 62, 140
Boucha, John, 47
Boucher (family) 75

Boulley (family) 77, 78
Boulley's Hill, 108, 109
Boulley, Ed, 33 (photo), 47, 114
Boulley, Norman, 109
Bourassa (family), 75
Boyer, Dan, 37, 60, 135, 138
Boyer, June, 37, 111
Brassar, 11, 59, 67, 91, 102, 103, 111, 119, 120, 158, 166
   Post Office, 97
Brassar (family), 75
Brassar Point, 57, 59, 86, 99, 119, (photo) 100
Brezavar, Floyd and Sarah, 118
bridges, 34, 35, 37, 38, 64, 65, 140-142, 149, 150-152
Brockway, Rev. William, 50
Brodeur, Fr. Ted, 157
Bryers, R.D. 173
Build-a-Road Day, 135-138
Bunday, Capt. Henry, 37
Bunker, Mae, 104
Burgess, Helen and Irv, 118

C
Cadotte, Polly, (photo) 115, 128
Cadreau (family) 40, 77
Cadreau, Alex, 135
Cadreau, James, 136
Cairns, Kathy, 159
Cairns, Mary (photo), 94
Cass Expedition, 32
Cass, Senator Lewis, 19
causeway, 30, 57, 64, 65, 85, 149, 152, 167
Causley, Pete, 57
census records, 71, 73, 75, 77, 101, 144
Chippewa ferry (photo) 60-62
Chippewa County Board of
   Supervisors) 34, 35, 42, 44, 46, 77, 85, 135, 138, 172
Chippewa County Road
   Commission, 14, 54, 62, 65, 67, 69, 85, 149, 151
Chippewa Indians, 17, 19, 20, 32, 42, 50, 73, 77
Chippewa Resort, 95
Church's Landing (photos) 44, 45, 52
Church, Gordon, 83

Church, J. Wells, 33, 45, 74, 75, 83, 146, 148
Church, Philetus, 33, 42-45, 52, 73, 99, 100, 114, 119, 144, 146, (portrait) 147, 148, 172
Clegg, Everett, 136
Clevenger, Raymond (photo), 139
Cloverland Electric Co. 138, 140
Clyde, (photo), 36, 37, 74
Clyde's Hamburger Stand, 11, (photo) 60, 167
Community Center, 84, 126
compensating dam, 34, 133
Cook, Mr. and Mrs. Frank, 28
Corbiere, Joan King, 157
Corbiere, Wayne, 157
Cowan, Robert, 95
Cox, Blanche (photos), 94, 107
Crushier, Annie, 102
Curtis, Impi, 14, 87, 107
Curtis, Royce, 136, 139, 173
Currie, Albert, 14, 48
Currie, Don, 119
Currie, Ruth (photo), 94

D

Daun photo collection, 81, 163
Day (family), 75
DeLisle (family), 75
DeLisle, Alfred, 104, 105
DeLisle, Celina (photo), 94
DeLisle, Leo, 48, 55, (photo), 107, 135
DeLorme (family) 75
Deo, Jack, 146, 148
DeTour, 17, 37, 44, 46, 83
Delafield, Major Joseph, 17, 174
Desmoyer, Frank, 47
Dickerson, Freeman, 127
Doty, James, 32, 33
Dowling, Rev. E.J., 37, 38, 57
Drummond Island, 17, 36, 44, 66, 75, 85, 146, 156
Drury, Lloyd, 125
Drury, Evelyn, 125
Duck Lake, 41, 127
Dunbar and Sullivan Dredging Co., 23, 28
Dunbar, F.E., 29

E

Eagle, Tate, 56

East Neebish Rapids, 20, 21
Ecklund, Paul, 173
Edison School, 103-106, 108, 110, 111, 166
Edwards (family), 77
Edwards, Sophia, 47
Eliot, "Sonny", 14, 143
Elva, 37, (photo) 38, 39, 89

F

Ferro, 37, 39
ferry traffic, 144, 149
Finn Hall, 91, 96, 157, (photos) 161, 162, 164
Finnish settlement of island, 85-92
Foard, Thomas, 95
Fox, Hazel, (photo) 94, 119
Fox, Jack, 14, 48, 67
Fox, Ken, 125
Fox, Leonard, 110, 119
Fox, Reg, 60
France, Horace, 136
Franchere, Gabriel, 19
Franks, Jeff and Rebecca, 170
Freeborn, Reeta, 14, 48
French, Isabella, 95

G

Gagnieur, Rev. William 114-116, 154
Garden River Ontario, 42, 97, 100
Gardner, Charley (photo), 125
Gates, William, 127
Gem Island, 19, 20, 22, 25, 112-114
  cemetery, 112
Gilbert, M.C., 99
Glad Tidings, 37
Glengarry (photo), 21
Gravel hauling, 52-54, 137
Gravel (family), 75
Gravelle, Kim, 14, 157
Great Lakes Dredge & Dock Co., 64
Greensky, John, 127
Gurnoe (family), 77
Gurnoe, Angus, 14, 39, 108

H

Hadfield, Babs, Elsie, Josie (photo), 49
Hamilton, "Pud" (photo), 142
Hamilton, Bill, 14, 21, 26, 128, 141
Hadziak, Alice and Ed, 118
Harbor Island, 75
Harrington, John N., 173

178

Hart, Sen. Philip (photo), 142
Hatch (family), 77
Hatch, Fred, 49, 54, 55 (photo), 115
Hatch, Louis, 49, 54, 78, (photo) 79, 165
Hatch, MaryAnne, 49, (photo) 79
Hay Lake channel, 22, 24, 26-28, 32-35, 37, 39, 77, 81
Heino(family), 89
Heller, Edith, 125
Heller, Fred, 125, 136, 140
Hickler, Henry, 45
Hickler, John, 45
Hilltop Bar, 11, 65, (photo) 125, 126, 140, 167, 168, 170
Hokkanen, Larry, 39, (photo) 90, 91, 92, 174
Hokkanen, Sylvia, (photo) 86, 90, 91
Holdsworth, Harry, 134 (photo), 133
Holli, Elsie, 89
Holt, Jack, 146
Holy Angels Church, 111
Homestead, 76, 118
  Post Office, 97
Homestead Act, 47
Hovey, Sylvia, 14, 55, 86, 100, (photo) 109, 110, 122, 158
Hughes, Eileen, 118
Hulbert, John, 127
Hunt, Marshall, 14, 39
Hunt, Maurice, 131
Husband, F.H., 95
Hytinen, Emil, 96, 119
Hytinen, Emma (photo), 94

I
ice harvesting, 54, 55
ice dam, 133

J
Joe Pete, (book) 93, 95, 114, 152-154
Johnson, Robert, 173
Johnston, John, 72
Jonas Island, 17
Jones, Benjamin, 111
Joseph, John, 127
Juhala, Paul, 158, 170

K
Kaikonnen, Esko, 135
Kangas, Sarah (photo), 94
Karelia (book), 91, 92, 174
Karimo, Lauri, 86, 110

Kauppi, Gert, 125
Kauppi, Gwen, 87
Keko, John, 87, (photo) 88, 89, 96
Keko, Milja, 87, 89
Kelcher, Lavina, 104
Kelley, Margaret, 104
Kemp, Ernie, 15
Kemp, George, 127
Kibble, Holly, 157
Kibby, Elmo, 37, 57, 58, 67, 86, 87, 95
King, Anna, (photo) 94
King, Linda and William, 125
Kinney, Mrs. W., 102
Kinney, Walter, (photo) 90
Korpi, Ella and Elsie, 105
Koski, Toivo, (photo) 90
Kraai, Helen Burgess, 118
Kuusisto, Andrew (photos) 90, 124
Kuusisto, Arvo (photo), 90
Kuusisto, Frank, 91

L
LaCoy (family), 67, 77, 114
Lake George, 11, 15, 17-26, 34, 42, 51, 54, 56, 87, 92, 112, 117, 131
  lighthouse in, 25
Laramie (family), 56, 75
  Post Office, 97, 98
  school, 108
Laramie, Abe, 4, 14, 55, 56, 99, 109
Laramie, Albert, 55, 97
Laramie, Delia, 97, 99
Lawless, Rev. Joseph, 14, 116
Leask (family), 75
Leask, Alfred, (photos) 83, 84
Leask, Dolly, (photo), 94
Leask, Joe, 119
Leask, Leona, (photo), 94
Leora M., 37
Levin, Louis, 65, 66
Levoines (family), 75
Lighthouse Service, 25, 76, 77
Lillie M. H., (photo) 41
Lime Island, 62, 155
Little Rapids, 15, 18, 19, 27, 30-34, 51, 56, 64, 77, 133, 141, 149
  charts, 27, 30
Little Rapids Cut, 31, 56, 64, (photo) 132

M
MacGilivry, Hector, 108
Maki, Oscar, 86

179

Maleport, Adelore, 57
Maleport, Armour (photo), 107
Maleport, Barbara, Beth, Dale, (photo) 94
Maleport, Bernice, 52
Maleport, Evelyn, 94
Maleport, Henry, 89
Maleport, Marie (Mrs. Emery), 57, 89, 99, (photo) 94
Maleport, Marie (Mrs. Adelore), 94
Maleport, Pete, 94, (photo) 107, 136
maple sugar, 17, 50
Marks, Bill, 14, 105
Marks, George and Mary Ellen, 14, 41
Marks, Harry, 41, 127
Marriott, A.E., 95
Masta (family), 75
May, John Wesley, 95
McClinchey, Florence, 93, 95, 152, 154, (photo) 155
McCoy, Daniel, 173
McCoy, Angus, 102, 119
McCoy, Irene, 14, 125
McCoy, Merlin, (photo) 124, 125, 126, 140
McFarlane Store (photo), 119
McFarlane, Donald and Harriet, 119
McFarlane, Harriet (photo) 94
McFarlane, John, 119
McIntosh, Elisha, Earline, Lucy, (photo) 94
McKechnie, Mary, 104
McKenzie, Pearl (photo) 107
McKerchie, Bert, 54, 110
McKerchie, Earl, 137
McKerchie, Anita, 159
McKerchie, Eric, 173
McMahon, Charles, 67, 173
Menard, Burt, 157
Menard, "Chum", 84
Menard, Joe, 11, 14, 100, 157
Menard, Pearl and Al, 157
Menard, Rose, 83, 100, 157
Mendoskin (family), 77
Methodist Mission, 32, 51
Michigan Home Mission Society, 116
Middle Neebish Channel, 39
 Rapids, 27, 28, 29
Miller, Steve, 126
Miller, Ward J., 95
Minisheing, 112
Minnedosa (photo) 21

Mohr, Harold, 173
Morley, Jon, 173
Murray (family), 108
Murray, Leonard, (photo) 107
Murray, Mary, 14, 49, 77-79, (photo) 80, 81, 102, 114, 136, 137
Murray, William, 173
Myerscough, Derek, 173
Myotte (family), 75

N

Native American, 17, 73, 116, 152, 154, 162
 population figures, 71
Nature, Mother, 37, 133
Naugatuck, (photo), 63
Neon, 37
Neebeetung, 32, 33
Neebish Island, 17, 27, 31, 76, 139, 156
Neebish Rapid, 18, 20, 21, 27, 28, 32
Neebish Rock Cut, 149
Nelson, Gil, 77, 128, 134, 135, 138 (photos) 140, 141, 142, 143
Nightingale, Urban, 97
Niles, William, 95
Niskanen, Henry, 89
Niskanen, Susan (photo), 94
Norris, "Hobie", 119, 123, 136
Norris, Jane, 119, 123

O

Oller, Freddie, 109
Olesek, Jennylee, 7, 14, 44, 45, 146, 147
Orasma (family), 89
Orasma, John, 110
Ord, Placidus, 99
Osborn Preserve, 41, 125-127, 162
Osborn, Chase S., 125-129, 130
Osborn, George, 127
Osborn, Stellanova, 129
Oshauguscodaywayqua, 71, 72

P

Packet, 28 (photo), 29
Palmer (family), 75
Palmer, Herb, 60
Patton, Michael, 173
Palmer, William, 172
Payment, 21, 37, 39, 79, 97, 99, 100, 103, 111, 112, 116, 157
 Post Office, 98
Payment (family), 143, 144

180

Payment, Alexis, 73
Payment, Alfred, 73
Payment, Francis Xavier, 37 (photo), 74
Payment, Frank, 52
Payment, Harriet (photo) 74
Payment, Joseph, 74
Payment, Michael G., 73, 99, 111, 157
Payment, Moses, 74
Payment, Philbert, 74
Payment, Susan, 74, 175
Payment, Victoria, 101
Payne & Dolan, 149, 151
Pearce logging camp, (photo) 53
Pearce, Charlie, 52, 98, 108
Pearce, Ed, 52
Pearce, Elmer, 98
Peck, Susan E., 22, 31, 81 (photos), 23, 24
Peer, Yvonne and Ron, 157
Penney, E.J., 52
Perrault, Dan, 80
Perrault (family), 75
Perrault, Edward, 47, 114
Perrault, Joseph, 114
Perrault, MaryAnne, 79
Peterman, E.E., 59, 60, 62
Phillips, Betty Lou, (photo) 115
Pilon, Roger, 11, 14, 45
Pim, Connie, 167
Pim, Jim, 158
Pine, Ed, 14, 33, 47, 51, 78, 111, 136
Pine, Mary, (photo) 78
Pink, E.J., 101
Pioneer, 33, 44
Piquette, Jack, 54
Pitezel, Rev. John, 32, 34, 175
Poirier Marine Co., 62
population figures, 172
Post Offices, 97-99
Povey, David, 95
Preslan, (photo) 50
Preslan, George, 52
Prud'homme, Rev. Paul, 116
Puddefoot, Rev. W.G., 116, 175
Purgatory Point, (photo) 142, 143

R
Rains, Allen, 21, 24, 75-77, 118, 144, 173
Rains, Norman, 21, 76
Rains, Owen, 31
Rains, William Kingdom, 76

Randall, Charles P., 127
range lights, 24, 25, 76
Reining, Sandy, 157
Rekola, Sulo, (photo), 90
Rich, Leo, 157
roads, 34, 57, 67, in 1931, (map), 68
Rogers, Allie, 14, 54
Roosevelt School, 103, 107, 110
Roussain, John, 173
Roy, Dorothy, (photo) 94
Roy, Rick, 173
Roy, Virginia, 14, 104, 105, 108
Roy, Wilfred, 173
Ruona, Tauno, 60
Rupp, Rev. N. Daniel, 112, 175

S
Saari, August, 47
Saari, Edward, 173
Saari, Reino, (photo) 90
Sabin, L.C., 95
Sacred Heart Church, 115, 116
Salo (family), 89
Sanderson, C.G., 135
Sasso, Rosalee, 146, 147
Sault Ste. Marie, Ontario, 86, 133, 137
Saunders, Bill and Nancy, 14, 87-90, 142
Schacher, Susan, 157
school committee minutes, 100
school districts, 79, 100-103, 110, 111
Schoolcraft, Henry Rowe, 48, 50, 71, 72, 154, 175
Schultz, Charles, 127
Scurr, Rev., 117
Search, 37
Sebastian (family), 75
Sebastian, Melvin "Mooney" 14, 39, 97
Sebastian, David, 26
Sebastian, Dorothy, 14
Sebastian, John, 101, 102
Sebastian, William, 110
Secrest, Carl and Pauline, 14, 96, 123
Seibert, Jack and Lou, 117
Service (first ferry), 57 (photo) 58, 59
Schaeffer, Dr. Joseph, 118
Shawano (family), 77
Shields, James, 98
Shultz, Charles, 95, 126
Smith, Frances (photo), 94
Smith, Frank, 59
Snider, George, 14, 157
snow roller (photo), 69

181

snowplowing, 67, 135
Sokeri Saari (book), 85, 169
Solway, Mary, (photo) 94
Solway, Phil, 108
Sprague, William, 42
St. Clair River, 22
St. Joseph Church, (photo) 113, (Gem Island), 114
St. Luke's Church, (photo) 118
St. Mary, 21
Steere's Island, 27, 30, 79
Stephenson, Vera, (photo) 94
Stevens, Jim, 60
Stockade tavern, (photo) 122
Sudendorf, L, 95
Sugar Island Co-Operative Association, 92
Sugar Islander, (photos) 61-63
Sugar Island Historical Preservation Society, 157-159
Sugar Island Rapids, 27
Supe, Hadie, 95
Supervisor list 172-173
Swanson, Allan, 14, 158, 160, 161, 169
Sylvester, Leo, 136, 173

T
Tamminen, Bill, (photo) 90
Tate, Capt. David, 44,101
taxable property, 46, 172
Tebo, John, 47
Thibert (family), 75
Thibert, Ambrose (Gene), 40, 97, 104, 119, 122, 137
Thibert, Bertha, 119, (photo) 40
Thibert, Henry, 60
Thibert, Marie, 123
Thibodeau (family), 75
Thompson, Don, 125
Thompson, Mamie, (photo) 94
Tiihonen, Toby, 91
Townsend, Fred, 95
Transportation Authority, E.U.P., 14, 62, 144
Treaty of 1855, 73
 Fond du Lac, 71
 Ghent, 17

Paris, 17, 18
Washington, 72
Webster-Ashburton, 18
Treau, P.R., 95
Trombley, Frank, 136

U
United Nations, 18, 130-132, 140

V
Vuori(family), 130
Vuori, Alex, 14
Vuori, Frank, 87, 132

W
Wa-ba-keke, Chief, 81, (photo) 82
Walker, William, 87, 89, 98, 124, 173
Walling, Regis, 112, 175
Walz, Maggie, 85
Ware, Charles, 47
Warner Township, 46
Warner, Ebenezer, 42, 46
Weitzel Lock, 24
Wellbaum, Willa, 136
Wellington Transportation Co., 62
Wellington, John,14, 36, 59-63, 114
Weston, Frank, 127
Wheeler, E.S., 24
Whipple Point, 20, (photo) 51, 91, 92
Whipple, Capt. Amiel, 20
White, Peter, 33
Wilcox, Robert, 125
Wilds, Earlin, 123, (photo) 125
Wilds, Gert, 123, (photo) 137
Wiley, Helen Seymour, 77
Wiley, Merlin, 95
Williams, Gov. G. Mennen (photo), 137
Williams, Jennie, 165
Williams, John, 110
Willis, J,T., 136
Willis, Marvin, 173
Willwalk, 37, 103, 105, 108, 111, 116, 124, 157, 170
 Post Office, 98
Wilson (family), 75
Wilson, William, 172
W.P.A., 162-165

About the Author

Bernard Arbic grew up in Sault Ste. Marie, Michigan, having spent a good deal of time at the family cottage on Sugar Island. During high school years, his parents built a home on the northwest side of island, where his mother still lives. After graduating from college, he spent two years teaching mathematics and physics in a secondary school in Northern Nigeria, where he and his future wife, Colleen, met.

He has been a member of the Mathematics Faculty at Lake Superior State University for twenty-two years, with degrees from M.I.T., Bowdoin College, and the University of Wyoming. His hobbies include vegetable gardening, cross country skiing, and singing barbershop harmony. He and Colleen are the parents of three sons - Brian, Joel, and Daniel.

Author Bernard Arbic.

Made in the USA
Monee, IL
29 June 2020